The Kennedy Moment (Myriad [

'The Kennedy Moment is that rare and clever thing – a gentle and moving thriller.'

– Staunch Book Prize, 2019

'In lucid, persuasive prose Peter Adamson tells a truly gripping story about something profoundly important.'

– Literary Review

'Reads like an Elmore Leonard novel, only with more emotion and more depth. I was spellbound, in genuine suspense.'

– Adam Fifield, author A Mighty Purpose.

'I was captivated from the start and found it hard to put it down until I'd reached the last page. It is a book that will stay with you long after you've finished it.'

– NB Literary Quarterly

'It was that rare book which makes you feel sad when you finish it because the process of reading it has been so enjoyable.'

– Fionnuala McCredie

Facing out to sea (Sceptre, 1997)

'I was captivated by the atmosphere but it was the sheer thoughtfulness of this novel that interested me…one of the most consistently intelligent and fascinating novels about what goes on in people's minds that I've read for a long time. Quite mesmeric in its hold.'

– Margaret Forster

'It took me into a world I knew very little about and opened my eyes to its beauty and interest. What I especially admired was the way the characters were both representative of large ideas and yet also fully human … it's a huge achievement.'

– Alain de Botton

The Tuscan Master (Sceptre, 2000)

'A tender and joyous celebration, a book that shows that ordinary lives, half-successful lives, even failed lives, can be lit with glory. At the end I was weeping with happiness. A beautiful, subtle, and very loving book.'

– William Nicholson,
author of *Shadowlands* and the screenplay for *Les Misérables*

Short story

Sahel – Winner of the 2013 Royal Society of Literature V. S. Pritchett Memorial Award for 2013. Available as a free e-book via Amazon.co.uk

LANDSCAPE IN TIME

THE WORLD OF THE
WITTENHAM CLUMPS

Peter Adamson

P&LA

First published 2021 by P&LA
© Peter Adamson (b. 1946), 2021
The moral right of the author has been asserted
https://peteradamsonwriting.com

ISBN 978-1-5272-7874-5

A catalogue record for this book is available from the British Library.

Designed and typeset in Minion by Charlie Webster,
Production Line, Minster Lovell, Oxford

Cover artwork and design by Rod Craig (www.rodcraig.com)

Printed and bound by Short Run Press, Exeter, England

Illustration: Sarah Woolfenden

For Anya, Petra, and Eleni
May your world be just as wonderful

THE WITTENHAM CLUMPS

Round Hill *(photograph: Andy Hough)*

Fort Hill *(author photograph)*

Brightwell Barrow *(photograph: Andy Hough)*

... haste can do nothing with these hills. I knew when I had looked for a long time that I had hardly begun to see.

Nan Shepherd, *The Living Mountain*

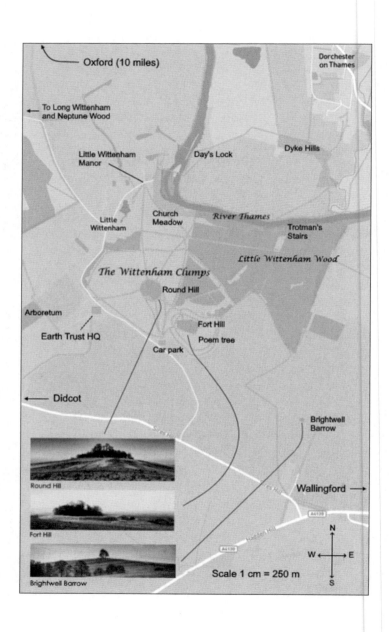

Oxford (10 miles)

Dorchester on Thames

To Long Wittenham and Neptune Wood

Little Wittenham Manor

Day's Lock

Dyke Hills

Little Wittenham

Church Meadow

River Thames

Trotman's Stairs

Little Wittenham Wood

The Wittenham Clumps

Round Hill

Arboretum

Earth Trust HQ

Fort Hill

Poem tree

Car park

Didcot

Brightwell Barrow

Round Hill

Wallingford →

Fort Hill

A4130

N

Brightwell Barrow

Hadden Hill

A4130

W ← → E

Scale 1 cm = 250 m

S

Contents

I. A step away from a story

Contents

CONTENTS

III. THE POINT OF DAFFODILS

IV. THE CHANGES THAT THE LAND BEFELL

Introduction

The two hills are so small that were they to be found in the Lake District or the Brecon Beacons they would probably not even have a name. But rising from the flat plain of South Oxfordshire and crowned by their distinctive stands of beech, the Wittenham Clumps are a well-known and well-loved local landmark.

I grew up with a very different sense of place – in a suburb of Leeds called Harehills where there were neither hares nor hills and the only green to be seen was on buses or lamp posts. But even though I have since been lucky enough to live for half a century within a mile or two of the Wittenham Clumps, I have to confess that for most of those years I paid them little attention. My working life, spent mostly with UNICEF and other agencies of the United Nations, took me all over the world but left me with no time to explore the world on my own doorstep. In the meantime, the Clumps and their surrounding fields, woods and river banks were gradually being acquired by the Earth Trust and opened to the public, offering miles of trails over chalk downs and wetlands, woodlands and water meadows.

Gradually, as the pace of work and travel slowed, I began to spend more time on the Earth Trust lands, enjoying the changing moods and passing seasons, sometimes strolling the broad grassy paths, sometimes pushing myself up one or other of the two hills that rise all of sixty-five metres above the Thames. Often on these walks, the thought occurred that I knew almost nothing about all that is to be seen of interest and intrigue, of beauty and strangeness, and of human activity and history from these two low hills that, a century ago, Paul Nash described as 'the pyramids of my

Round Hill   Fort Hill   Brightwell Barrow

The Clumps *(illustration: Scott Johnson)*

small world'. Often, also, was I was reminded of that line in Philip Larkin's poem '*Churchgoing*' – 'Someone would know: I don't'. Today, that someone is often generous enough to make his or her knowledge available on-line. And so curiosity slipped into research on the stories and the secrets that this landscape, its views and its dwelling places, have to tell.

The result is this collection of essays on the world of the Wittenham Clumps. I hope it may add to the interest and enjoyment of others who walk this way, and of all who delight in the stories that the landscapes of our extraordinary country have to offer.

Peter Adamson

Acknowledgements

Landmark in Time owes its greatest debt to all those who have uploaded their knowledge to the many websites consulted.

As always, I am grateful to my partner, Lesley Adamson, who suggested many ideas, commented on every chapter as it was written, and offered unfailingly valuable criticism. As with previous books, my thanks also go to Candida Lacey, Publishing Director of Myriad Editions, and John Marzillier, both of whom gave perceptive advice and encouragement as the work progressed.

I should also like to thank the following for their support and help with individual chapters: Christopher Baines, Angie Bowden, Kathleen Burk, Robin Buxton, Anna Dillon, Philip Errington, Janet Haylett, Graham and Sonia Hobbins, Andrew Hutt *(The Berkshire Archaeological Journal)*, Carol Hurley, Gabriel Hemery (Sylva Foundation), Bill Horsfield, Andrew Lea, Colin Nicolson, Revd David Rice, Peter Rose, Fiona Smart (Harwell Science Campus) and Chris Warrick (Culham Science Centre).

Special thanks are due to Rod Craig who generously painted *The Wittenham Clumps* for the cover of *Landmark in Time*. A two-minute video of the painting being created can be viewed at https://bit.ly/3kwgXQI. More of Rod Craig's artwork can be viewed at www.rodcraig.com.

My thanks also to Sarah Woolfenden for permission to include the illustrations on the title pages of Parts I–IV of *Landmark in Time*. More fine work by Sarah, available as prints and greetings cards, can be viewed at www.sarahwoolfenden. co.uk.

ACKNOWLEDGEMENTS

Many thanks also to Anna Dillon, Andy Hough, Scott Johnson and Colin Smith for permission to include their photographs and illustrations.

Finally my thanks also to Charlie Webster, scourge of widows and orphans and master of the dark arts of making plain text look good.

❧

The title page quotation from *The Living Mountain* © Nan Shepherd, 1977 is reproduced by kind permission of Canongate Books Ltd.

The quotation from *The Old Ways: A Journey on Foot* is included by kind permission of the author, Robert Macfarlane. The quotation from Alain de Botton is included by kind permission of Alain de Botton

Quotations from *The Immense Journey* by Loren Eiseley are reproduced by kind permission of the publisher, Random House, an imprint and division of Penguin Random House LLC.

Quotations from *The Ash and the Beech* by Richard Mabey © Vintage (2013). are reproduced by kind permission of Sheil Land Associates Ltd.

Quotations from the writings of John Masefield are included by kind permission of The Society of Authors (Literary Representative of the Estate of John Masefield). Quotations from *John Masefield's Great War*, edited by Philip W. Errington, are included by kind permission of the publisher, Pen & Sword Military, (1st Edition 2007).

Every attempt has been made to obtain the necessary permissions for use of copyright material. Apologies are offered for any omissions; future editions will include appropriate acknowledgement.

I

A STEP AWAY FROM A STORY

Illustration: Sarah Woolfenden

... a walk is only a step away from a story, and every path tells.

Robert Macfarlane, *The Old Ways: A Journey on Foot*

1

A LANDMARK IN TIME

Probably it was a peaceful spring or autumn morning in the early 1740s that the villagers of Little Wittenham set about planting the saplings that became the Wittenham Clumps, no doubt grumbling at having to labour up the two hills to indulge an aristocratic fad. Those original beech trees are long gone. But new growth and replanting have meant that the Clumps today are the oldest surviving example of the eighteenth-century fashion for 'adding distinction to the landscape' by planting groups of trees in prominent places.

By comparison with today, the world of those labourers and landowners must have seemed timeless. Only in the previous century had feudalism breathed its last, long expiring breath, and in rural England there was still much that was mediaeval. But what neither labourer nor landowner could have known at the time was that the planting of the Clumps marked the moment when the land they looked down upon was about to lead the world into the modern era.

Just across the Thames, in the village of Crowmarsh Gifford, the ground for the Agricultural Revolution was being prepared by Jethro Tull's invention of the horse hoe and the rotating-cylinder seed drill. Along with new farming methods like 'Turnip' Townsend's system of crop rotation, such changes would almost double the productivity of the land – and the population of England – in less than a century. Before long, the fields around the Wittenham Clumps were being hedged and fenced into enclosures that meant record yields for landowners and much suffering for the rural poor.

Meanwhile, in the Midlands, the North and in Wales, Abraham Darby's coke-powered blast furnaces were turning out pig iron and James Watt was inventing the rotary steam engine that would wake the clanking giant of the industrial revolution. Manufacturing, it seemed, had become a craze; as the Dean of Gloucester said at the time, no doubt shaking his head at the neglect of godliness for worldly pursuits, 'everyone hath a new invention of his own and is daily improving on the work of others'.

For the first time, also, Britain's towns and cities were being linked up by thousands of miles of new turnpikes along which wagons and sprung-frame stagecoaches were carrying both people and goods. In the early 1740s, only one coach a day was travelling between London and Birmingham; twenty years later, two were leaving every hour.

In religion, politics and culture, the country of those first saplings was also taking on a recognisably modern stamp. The 'Divine Right of Kings' was passing into history; in its place, Britain's first Prime Minister, the overweight country squire Robert Walpole, was munching apples in the House of Commons and guiding the nation towards government by Parliament and Cabinet. Soon, too, 'popery' would also be gone. Within a year or two of the Clumps being planted, the threat of a return to Catholicism would bleed to death on the battlefield of Culloden; from now on, Britain was to be a Protestant country under the Church of England, though Wesley's open-air preaching was gathering many into the Methodist fold.

Not far from where Walpole had decided to take up residence in Downing Street, language and literature were also entering a new phase as the fashion for coffee houses took hold. Richardson and Fielding were scratching out the first English novels, Gibbon was working on his six-volume *Decline and Fall of the Roman Empire,* and Samuel Johnson was compiling his famous *Dictionary of the English Language* (though it did not seem likely that English would one day become the language of much of the world: the first edition of the *Encyclopaedia Britannica*, published in Scotland at the time, noted that 'English is less known in every foreign country than any other language in Europe.')

In music and painting, too, a new world was emerging. Bach, Mozart and Haydn were touring Britain. Handel was composing in London. Turner, Constable, Gainsborough and Reynolds were painting rural idylls and portraits of the wealthy while the engraver William Hogarth shocked polite society by depicting the hardships of the poor. By the middle of the century, almost two thousand parishes had instituted workhouses to reduce the cost of poor relief: for the homeless elderly, workhouses were usually the end of the line; for their grandchildren, they were often a staging post on the way to the textile factories of Lancashire and the North.

All in all, by the time the Wittenham Clumps were reaching their prime, the country they looked down upon had become, as Daniel Defoe described it, 'the most flourishing and opulent country in the world'.[1] As a revealing detail of that flourishing, it was noted by a French traveller at the time that 'from Paris to St Petersburg, from Amsterdam to the farthest point of Sweden, from Dunkirk to the southern extremity of France, one is served at every Inn from English earthenware'.[2]

More fundamentally, the years when the Wittenham Clumps were growing to maturity were also years when ways of thinking were changing so profoundly as to be known today as the Age of Enlightenment. Led by a succession of enduringly influential thinkers – John Locke and Baron de Montesquieu, Tom Paine and Adam Smith, Marie Gouze and Mary Wollstonecraft, and eventually Jeremy Bentham and John Stuart Mill – the Enlightenment posited that observation, evidence and reason should replace irrational beliefs and traditions, that accountability should supplant arbitrary authority, and that 'the greatest good of the greatest number' should guide the conduct of public affairs. And at a time when women were regarded as little more than chattels, Marie Gouze and Mary Wollstonecraft were raising the first banners in the long struggle for emancipation.

The influence of these ideas on the world of today is nowhere more obvious than in the writings of the moral philosopher Adam Smith, who had just taken up residence ten miles north of the Clumps at Balliol College, Oxford. There he began developing the ideas that have dominated economic thinking ever since. Disappointed in a university which had 'given up altogether even the pretence of teaching,' he eventually returned to Scotland where other pioneers of the Enlightenment were coming together in what today would be called think-tanks – the Political Economy Club, the Select Society, the Poker Club. From Edinburgh and Glasgow in particular, the 'hotbeds of genius', their ideas would spread across the world (much like the game of golf whose rules were also being written at this time by the Gentlemen Golfers of Leith).

Perhaps of closer interest to the villagers of Little Wittenham, the Age of the Enlightenment was also the age of cotton underwear. Suddenly, it seemed, Lancashire's mass-produced cottons were everywhere. 'Women of all ranks, from the highest to the lowest,' noted Macpherson's '*Annals of Commerce*' in 1785, 'are clothed in British manufactured cottons, from the muslin cap on the crown of the head to cotton stockings under the sole of the foot, and for durability of colour, generally stand the washing so well as to appear fresh and new every time they are washed'. Also of interest to villagers everywhere, and possibly the cause of a few grumbles, was an Act of Parliament, passed in 1753, which decreed that all marriages had to be performed by a clergyman; until then, all that had been necessary was that a couple should freely exchange their marriage vows.

As for the wider world, these were the years when Captain James Cook was learning his seamanship on a Whitby collier, soon to embark on the first of the great voyages that would chart the southern hemisphere and complete the modern map of the world (the famous portrait of Cook in the National Maritime Museum at Greenwich was painted by Nathaniel Dance-Holland who lived just below the Clumps at Little Wittenham Manor). In passing, Cook would lay claim to New South Wales, and by extension Australia, adding to British possessions in North America and the Indian sub-continent. No surprise, then, that it was also at this time that the jingoistic strains of 'Rule, Britannia!' were first being heard fifty miles downstream at Cliveden.

All of this would no doubt have been of only distant concern to the villagers as they trudged up the two hills by the Thames, carrying those first saplings. Even less would they have been occupied by events in a distant colony where George Washington was qualifying as a land surveyor and Benjamin Franklin was inventing the lightning rod that would save many an English parish church from fire (although often resisted by the clergy on the grounds that attaching such a device to a church steeple showed a deplorable lack of faith). Fewer still would have been aware that, on average, every ring added to the annual growth of the beech trees on the Wittenham Clumps saw eighty thousand Africans being shackled and shipped over the Atlantic, half of them in British ships.

Taken together, such changes have led to a world that would be only partly intelligible to those eighteenth-century villagers. They would no doubt still recognise the contours of the land itself, and the gentle skyline of Chilterns and Downs. They would be familiar, too, with the squat mediaeval tower of Little Wittenham's Parish Church. And as they looked up from the Clumps, wondering at the strange silvery comets ploughing loosening white furrows across the skies, they would also recognise the red kites circling low over the hillside, though they would be surprised to know that they had become extinct and been re-introduced from foreign countries.

If, after work in the evening, they were to stroll down to the Thames today, they would find the old flash lock gone. Instead of the wooden gates which released a precarious flood to carry barges over the weir, they would see a tranquil tank with giant doors at both ends through which were passing not barges carrying timber, coal, potash, and malt, but sleek and shining craft, graceful and horseless, transporting picnic hampers and portable barbecues. If they were to linger on the Clumps after nightfall, they would see not a great darkness over all the land but more lights on earth than in the heavens. And should they be out and about in the early morning, they would hear not the sound of birdsong and cuckoos calling but a constant, faint swish of tyres on the A4074, sounding for all the world like wind in the trees.

Even excluding the most obvious signs of change – from the gantries of the electrified Great Western railway to the distant glint of sun on the BMW factory at Cowley – there are changes to the world of the Clumps that the surrounding villagers might have found even more deeply puzzling. Most of all, they would surely have asked – why is nobody working? And who are these oddly dressed men and women walking their strange-looking dogs to and fro to no apparent purpose? And why so few wildflowers, animals, birds, bees, butterflies, insects? Where are the jewel beetles and tortoiseshell butterflies? Where the lapwings and the curlews, the shrikes and flycatchers, the cuckoos and nightjars, the linnets and skylarks, the bullfinches and yellow-hammers, the turtle doves and brown owls, the corncrakes and meadow pipits, the merlins and hobbies and the over-wintering hen harriers? Where the fritillaries and cornflowers, the rabbits and hares, the field mice and hedgehogs, the otters and water voles, foxes and badgers, ferrets and polecats? [3]

The answers lie in other sights that would stun the eighteenth-century villager: the two-hundred-horsepower tractor ploughing a fifty-acre field in less time than a farmer leading a horse could turn over a single furrow; the enormous span of insect-like arms being dragged across the land to spray a mist over a whole field in just a few passes; the dense acres of wheat growing no more than knee-high but bearing a much heavier head of grain; the combine-harvester reaping, threshing, winnowing and binding eighty acres in a single day; the straight hedgerows dividing up the fields and the lack of any land left fallow.

Perhaps most puzzling of all would be the emptiness of the countryside. Cumulatively, the inventions, ideas and explorations that began around the time of the Clumps have brought a change from a world where almost everybody worked on the land to a world where almost nobody does. At the same time, the yield from that land has increased beyond the imaginings of the eighteenth century. But at a price. And that price includes the burden of chemical pesticides that have made these fertile fields of wheat, barley, rapeseed and legumes into a desert for other forms of life.

Something important, then, has been lost in all that has been gained since the first planting of these trees. But it is easy to lament the present and sentimentalise the past, especially so when that past is so often portrayed as an unchanging idyll, free of pollution and stress. It should perhaps also be remembered that it was only in the previous century that Thomas Hobbes had described the natural condition of human life as 'solitary, poor, nasty, brutish and short'.

This, then, was the world on which the newly planted trees of the Wittenham Clumps looked down. Today, almost three centuries later, they have become a landmark in time – a living marker of the beginning of the modern world.

2

THE RIGHT STUFF

Many who walk the Wittenham Clumps will have looked down on the village of Little Wittenham and assumed that its stone tower is the parish church. In fact, the tower of St. Peter's is screened by its ancient yew tree; the tower seen from the Clumps is a twentieth-century addition to Little Wittenham's Manor house.

Dating back to the sixteenth century and rebuilt in the eighteenth, the Manor has stood at the heart of the village for almost five hundred years. In the 1980s, it became the home of Sir Martin and Lady Audrey Wood, founders and benefactors of the Earth Trust – an environmental charity that owns the Wittenham Clumps and much of the surrounding land. But at the beginning of the twentieth century, the Manor had a very different kind of connection with the environmental cause.

Step forward Apsley George Benet Cherry-Garrard, who in the year 1907 inherited Little Wittenham Manor and all its estates, including the Wittenham Clumps and Wittenham Woods.

In many ways, Cherry-Garrard is an unsympathetic figure. Educated at Winchester and Oxford, he had drunk deep of the notion that the English are superior to all other nationalities and members of his own class superior to all other Englishmen. Not having to work for a living himself, he disliked the newly assertive working classes, drove a coach-built Mulliner Rolls Royce with the family crest emblazoned on the doors, and grumbled interminably about Lloyd George's land taxes. Yet for all the high-Tory baggage and never-trust-Johnny-foreigner attitudes, it is impossible not to admire the spirit of adventure that took the twenty-four-year-old Cherry-Garrard from the soft sheets and servants of his inherited estates to the hardships and teeth-shattering cold of the Antarctic, where he sailed with Captain Scott in 1910. Impossible, also, not to feel some sympathy for the guilt that haunted him for the rest of his life over the decision he took, alone, two years later, on the edge of the Great Ice Barrier.

༻ॐༀ

Cherry-Garrard was just twenty-one when he inherited Lamer Park in Hertfordshire and the estates of Denford and Little Wittenham in Berkshire. Choosing to live at Lamer Park, he retained a land agent, collected his rents, travelled a little, and wondered what to do with his life.

Like many young men of his generation, Cherry-Garrard had absorbed Scott's account of his first expedition to the Antarctic. When he heard that the famous explorer was preparing to return for an attempt on the South Pole, he worked his contacts and made his application. The problem was that more than eight thousand other young Englishmen had the same idea. And most of those who volunteered had more skills and better eyesight than the spectacle-wearing Cherry-Garrard. Despite the backing of Wilson, Scott's chief scientific advisor, his application was turned down. He then decided to offer a donation of £1,000 (perhaps £50,000 in today's money) towards the cost of the expedition if Scott would reconsider his application. Scott again turned him down. Cherry-Garrard made the donation anyway. Impressed, Scott agreed to a meeting. According to Wilson, 'the sparkle in his eye clinched it', and Cherry-Garrard was taken onto the expedition strength as one of two 'adaptable helpers'. The other was another wealthy young Lord of the Manor, Lawrence Edward Grace Oates, who was to enter into legend by walking out into a blizzard rather than become a burden to his companions, famously telling Scott, 'I am just going out. I may be some time.'

One condition was that Cherry-Garrard had to learn to operate a typewriter, there being no one else who could use such a machine to keep a record of the expedition. Of greater concern was that he would also have to take his turn at cooking on a primus stove. Having never so much as boiled an egg in his life, and being accustomed to having hot water brought to him by a maid, Cherry-Garrard startled the below-stairs staff at Lamer Park by appearing in the kitchens in search of lessons.

Some in Scott's party wondered about the inclusion of a young man so lacking in either skills or experience, and it was murmured that perhaps he was being taken along because his Greek and Latin might come in handy at the Pole. But he was to surprise them all. After only a few weeks in the Antarctic, Scott wrote in a letter home: 'Cherry-Garrard has won all hearts. He shows himself ready for any kind of hard work and is always to the front when the toughest jobs are on hand ... I hope you will let his people know what golden opinions he has deserved and won.'

Scott also noticed that Cherry, as he came to be known to his companions, seemed to be happy in the Antarctic. 'I haven't asked him if he is,' he wrote, 'but when I see his cheerful brown face charged with enthusiasm and wreathed in smiles I cannot doubt it, but indeed it is a good life for any young man who has the right stuff in him.' Bill Wilson had the same impression: 'I really never have seen anyone,' he wrote, 'with such a constant expression of 'this is what I have been looking for' on his face.'

It was not to last. The physical toll of the hardships he endured in the Antarctic, and the mental toll taken by what happened at One Ton Depot in March 1912, were to weigh heavily on his spirits for the rest of his life, provoking bouts of mental instability and mummifying depression.

What almost saved him was a commission from the Antarctic Publications Committee to write the official account of Scott's expedition. At first, he worked at this in the peace of his estates at Lamer Park. But in endlessly revising the outline of the proposed book he gradually realised that it was not lists of equipment or the best length for sledge runners that interested him. Having ample means to go his own way, he eventually broke with the Antarctic Committee and instead turned for advice to his next-door neighbour who, as fortune would have it, happened to be George Bernard Shaw.

The result was *The Worst Journey in the World*, often described as 'the greatest travel book ever written'. Privately printed in 1922, *The Worst Journey* was an instant classic. The *Evening Standard* acclaimed it as 'the most wonderful story in the world'. *The Bookman* went further, announcing that it was 'scarcely decent' to publish a review as it was 'more seemly to salute such a book with the ancient greeting of the Roman, standing with outstretched, uplifted arm in silent admiration of great men and great deeds recorded'.

❦

The 'worst journey' of the book's title was not Scott's nine-hundred-mile march to the South Pole, but the side trip made the previous year by Cherry and his two great heroes, Edward 'Uncle Bill' Wilson and Henry 'Birdie' Bowers.

Setting out in the mistaken belief that the embryo of an emperor penguin would be a major contribution to Darwinian science, proving the evolutionary link between birds and reptiles, the three men ventured out from Scott's base camp into the permanent night of an Antarctic winter. It was to be a five-week trip across the Great Ice Barrier in an attempt to reach the only place on the planet where emperor penguins incubate their young.

Deciding not to take any of the expedition's precious dogs, Cherry, Wilson and Bowers man-hauled their supplies in temperatures that soon fell below minus-fifty degrees Fahrenheit. On mid-winter's night, June 22nd, 1911, Cherry noted in his diary 'A hard night: clear, with a blue sky so deep that it looks black: the stars are steel points: the glaciers burnished silver. The snow rings and thuds to your footfall.'

Two weeks in, the thermometer showed minus-sixty. Day and night were now meaningless. Ice ridges and crevasses appeared out of the darkness. The sun never rose, and they steered by Jupiter. 'I never see him now,' wrote Cherry later, 'without recalling his friendship in those days.'

Another week and the temperature dropped to minus seventy-five. Almost all of Cherry's teeth split. When the three men stopped to rest, it took an hour to remove enough ice to get into their sleeping bags. When they awoke, the bags were crumpled steel. Before leaving the tent, they had to crouch into their pulling positions as, once outside, it took only seconds for their clothes to become suits of armour. The blisters on Cherry's hands were frozen solid.

For five weeks, the menu consisted of three items: butter, which splintered under the knife; biscuits specially made by Huntley & Palmer, and pemmican – a compressed cake of fats and protein originally invented by Native Americans. If they could get the primus stove to light and wait for an hour, they had tea, which Wilson said was 'like putting a hot water bottle to your heart'.

Reading Chapter Seven of Cherry's *The Worst Journey in the World* is enough to make anyone snuggle down under a duvet with a copy of *Under the Tuscan Sun*. But Cherry gives the impression that it was just a matter of recalibrating what one means by 'cold'. 'We began to look upon minus fifties,' he wrote, 'as a luxury we did not often get.'

Much of the chapter is taken from Cherry's own diary of the trip, though there were times when even breathing on a sheet of paper saw it instantly covered in a film of ice on which no pencil could make an impression. And it was a diary written in the darkness, for the sun never rose. To Cherry, the perpetual dark was almost as hard to endure as the cold. 'I don't believe minus seventy temperatures would be bad in daylight,' he wrote, 'when you could see where you were going.'

On July 15th, 1911, they heard the first metallic cries of the emperor penguins on the wild shores of Cape Crozier and found themselves looking with dismay down the ice cliff that separated them from the breeding ground below. But they had come through too much to give up now, and by roping themselves through crevasses and ice tunnels, they managed to descend to where the penguins were huddled together on the sea ice, each with a single egg balanced under a tuft of feathers on webbed feet.

Returning to the cliff top with three of the eggs, they sensed a blizzard building in the darkness. They constructed walls of ice, spread their tent over the top, and settled in just before the full force of the blizzard struck. 'The indescribable fury and roar of it all,' wrote Cherry, 'cannot be imagined.' All three knew that they were unlikely to survive. And what hope they had vanished when the tent was torn away into the Antarctic night. For two days and two nights they lay in the open, their sleeping bags becoming coffins. Bowers and Wilson sang hymns into the howling wind. Cherry peered out into the darkness, occasionally glimpsing the black Antarctic ocean in the distance. Their position, he later wrote, 'was not altogether a comfortable one'.

After forty-eight hours the blizzard blew itself out and they were able to lever themselves from their bags. When they peered around, they could not believe what they saw. Less than half a mile away lay a bundle of green canvas, frozen into the ice by bamboo poles. The three men stared at each other, knowing that the tent was the difference between life and death.

When they arrived back at Hut Point base almost three weeks later, carrying the three penguin eggs, Scott noted in his diary: 'The Crozier party returned last night after enduring for five weeks the hardest conditions on record. They looked more weather-worn than anyone I have yet seen. Their faces were scarred and wrinkled, their eyes dull, their hands whitened and creased.'

Cherry also made a diary entry that night: 'Then into my warm blanket bag, and I managed to keep awake just long enough to think that Paradise must feel something like this.'

అచ్చా

From the point of view of science, the journey to Cape Crozier proved futile. But that was not what mattered to Cherry. What mattered was that he had stood the test of what even Scott described as 'the hardest journey ever made'. What mattered was that he had behaved, again according to Scott, 'exactly as the best sort of Englishmen behaved on such occasions'. And what mattered most of all was the bond forged between himself and the companions for whom his admiration knew no limits. Wilson and Bowers had remained good-tempered and cheerful even when death seemed certain. In Cherry's view, 'these two men were gold, pure, shining, unalloyed'.

And this was why he could never forget, and never forgive himself for, that day fifteen months later when he was to drag open a frozen tent to find the bodies of Wilson and Bowers, their skin the colour of alabaster, lying like ice-sculptures on either side of Scott.

Cherry's return to England was not a happy one. The House of Lords had been humbled by Lloyd George's Liberals and the landed classes were under attack. War with Germany was imminent. And he had lost the friends he had come to love. What should have been the high point of his return seemed to sum up the disillusionment. Acutely conscious of representing his lost companions, he went along to the British Museum to offer the three precious emperor penguin eggs. After being made to wait for some time in a corridor, he was seen by a junior assistant who took the eggs from him with some reluctance and little thanks. Later, when he escorted one of Scott's sisters on a visit to see the eggs for which he, Bowers and Wilson had made 'the worst journey in the world', the museum denied ever having received them.

He volunteered, of course, for service on the Western Front. Not knowing quite where he fitted in, he thought to use his Antarctic experience by training dogs to find wounded soldiers on the battlefield. When this came to nothing, he served in the ranks as a motorcycle dispatch rider. But this, too, ended unhappily. Soon after arriving at the Front, he was invalided home suffering from the ulcerative colitis he had developed in the Antarctic cold. Back at Lamer Park, he resumed the tedious business of dealing with tenants and land agents and attending to 'school repairs' and 'problems of sanitation' on his estates at Little Wittenham. Out shopping one day, the man who had faced so much danger was presented with a white feather.

Few interests could stir him now, though eventually he roused himself sufficiently to join the Home Guard where he was forced to ask permission to parade in slippers because of his swollen, painful feet.

With his investments prospering and rents continuing to flow in from his estates at Denford, Lamer and Little Wittenham, as well as from his London home, he was now an even wealthier man. But it was little consolation. Time weighed heavily. And perhaps, also, his present life seemed tarnished by decadence after the purity and what he called the 'unowned-ness' of the Antarctic.

For a time, he was inspired by visits to his estate at Little Wittenham where, in that peaceful setting, he conceived the notion of building his ideal home. The site he chose was Trotman's Stairs on the banks of the Thames. Though the landing stage and its name have long ago disappeared from use, old maps reveal that it was at the bottom end of a glade in Wittenham Woods, today marked only by a memorial bench to a local schoolteacher and by the scattering of spotted orchids that bloom there in the spring.

❧

Initially, the commission to write the official account of Scott's expedition seemed like a lifeline for a man about to drown in despondency. But his enthusiasm faded when he realised that the Antarctic Publications Committee was going to insist on omitting anything that might be taken as criticism of the expedition, including his account of how it had all ended. 'The committee mean to hush up everything,' he wrote in his journal. When he raised the issue with the Committee's solicitor, he was told 'there must be no scandal.'

Resentment, and a private income, now moved him to decisiveness and he cut his links with the Committee, leaving himself free to tell the truth of the expedition as he saw it. But it was the neighbourly advice and the paragraph-by-paragraph questioning of George Bernard Shaw that gave him the confidence and the clarity to turn his account into a classic.

The second part of *The Worst Journey in the World* is Cherry's version of the story that used to be known to every school child. On November 1st, 1912, Scott, Wilson, Bowers, Oates and Evans left their base camp at Hut Point to traverse nine hundred miles of the most inhospitable terrain on the planet in an attempt to raise the Union Jack at the South Pole. Two and a half months later, on January 17th, 1913, they reached their goal. Waiting for them were the month-old sled tracks of the Norwegian, Amundsen, already fading away into the ice. 'All our day-dreams must go,' Scott confessed, as he contemplated a different red, white and blue flag flying from a small snow cairn at the Pole.

The five-man party then began the long struggle back across the Antarctic plateau. Temperatures plummeted. Progress slowed. Paraffin leaked away from faulty leather seals. Antarctic veteran Edgar Evans was the first to die. Four weeks later, frostbite having turned to a vicious gangrene, Titus Oates walked out into the blizzard.

Back at Hut Point base camp, plans were rapidly being changed. Atkinson, the expedition's surgeon, had orders to take a dog team south to One Ton Depot, one of many where food and paraffin had been buried in preparation for the return from the Pole. There he was to wait for the polar party and, with a fresh dog team, hasten their return so that the *Terra Nova* could sail before the ice froze, allowing Scott to send the news of his triumph to a waiting world. But Atkinson was dealing with a medical emergency, and it was decided that Cherry, despite his inexperience, should set out to meet the returning polar party. Winter was already closing in and the light beginning to fade when, on February 26th, 1912, Cherry and a Russian dog handler, Dimitri, set off on the one-hundred-and-thirty-mile journey across the Great Ice Barrier to One Ton Depot.

Confident that Scott would be ahead of schedule, Cherry expected the polar party to be waiting for them. They were not there.

Surprised to find that no dog food had been left with the rest of the supplies, Cherry now faced a dilemma. Without food for the dogs, they could only proceed further south by killing one dog at a time to feed the rest. But on that point, Scott's orders had been explicit: on no account were the dogs to be sacrificed, as they were needed for another winter of scientific exploration. In any case, Cherry reasoned, even if they did disobey orders and proceed further south there was every chance he would miss the returning polar party in the approaching blizzard. In the end, he decided to remain at One Ton Depot where an eventual meeting with Scott was more certain. The polar party was not yet overdue, and there was no reason to suppose that Scott was in trouble.

But Scott's party was in trouble. Oates and Evans were already dead. The surviving three – Scott, Wilson and Bowers – were frostbitten, snow-blinded, exhausted and almost out of food and fuel. The weather was worsening and they were still seventy miles from One Ton Depot.

When the blizzard struck, they were only a dozen miles from safety. But for the next nine days they were pinned down in the brutal cold, their supplies exhausted, life and hope ebbing away. Amputations were now certain, they knew. But survival might still be possible if, over the howls of the blizzard, they were to hear the cries of the dog team they believed was travelling south to meet them.

To the north, Cherry waited. And waited. After six days, with still no sign of Scott, he checked his supplies. He had just enough dog food to get back to base. On March 10th, he and Dimitri harnessed the dogs, left a note for Scott in a film canister, and turned back.

It was not until eight months later, after another Antarctic winter had passed, that Cherry was able to return with a search party. Eleven and a half miles south of One Ton Depot, they glimpsed through the gloom what looked like a small snow cairn. Approaching in silence, they saw the tell-tale green of a tent. When they had shovelled away the snow, Cherry dragged open the cambric flap. Inside were the marble effigies of Scott, Wilson, and Bowers. His diary entry reads: 'We have found them – to say it has been a ghastly day cannot express it – it is too bad for words.' Wilson, the man Cherry had worshipped, lay with his hands folded quietly across his chest. By Scott's head was a pouch of tobacco and a bag of tea.

They left the three bodies in their bags and collapsed the tent. Over it, they built a snow cairn topped with a cross of skis. It was almost midnight, the sun low over the South Pole, the cross silhouetted against a sky of blazing gold. Atkinson read a chapter from Corinthians. The words, Cherry said later, had never been read in a more magnificent cathedral – 'for it is a grave which kings must envy'.

✦✦✦

Back home, the topic being discussed in the editorial columns and over a thousand dinner tables was whether or not Scott could and should have been rescued. Why had Cherry not pressed on south for just a few miles more? Even some expedition members had begun referring to the dog team's journey to One Ton Depot as a 'relief mission' instead of merely a means of speeding up the polar party's return. Cherry's version of events was all but drowned out, leaving him, as he put it, 'in the dirt tub'.

The eventual success of *The Worst Journey in the World* helped to put the record straight. But the book was more than just an opportunity for Cherry to tell his side of the story. Probably under Shaw's influence, it went where few travel books had gone before. Such works were expected to burnish the image of the Empire and its heroes, glossing over flaws and failures. Instead, Cherry portrayed an enterprise that was, in many ways, ill-conceived, ill-planned and ill-led.

To begin with, the good ship *Terra Nova* was old, cumbersome and unsuitable for journeying through the Southern Ocean and the Antarctic pack-ice. Then there were the logistical failings: the poor nutritional quality of the rations, the ponies whose hooves sank deep into the snow, the leaky leather paraffin seals, the failure to check that dog food had been left at One Ton Depot. Worse were the confused orders that meant that Cherry believed he was to wait at One Ton when Scott expected him to continue on south to meet the returning polar party.

More fundamentally, Cherry revealed that the expedition had suffered from conflicting aims. Being the first to reach the South

Pole was what had captured the nation's imagination. It was the news that the sponsors and the public were waiting for and that the Empire expected. But the expedition's other sponsors, the Admiralty and the Royal Geographical Society, also demanded specimen collecting and rigorous scientific observation.

The conflict was apparent from the beginning. It was science that demanded starting out from Cape Evans rather than closer to the Pole. It was science that sent Cherry, Wilson and Bowers on their wild penguin chase through the dark of an Antarctic winter so that, as Wilson himself noted in his diary, 'the team that undertook the journey were taken to the limit even before the trek to the Pole had begun.' Perhaps most poignantly of all, it was science that weighed down Scott's sledges with rock samples even as he struggled back on that last terrible journey across the Antarctic plateau.

Cherry himself had no doubt which was the more important of the two aims. In his mind, they had travelled in the name of science. The emperor penguin embryos from Cape Crozier, the fossils they had collected from Buckley Island, and the rock and plant samples collected in freezing dark or howling winds, were brought back so that, as Cherry put it, 'the world may have a little more knowledge, that it may build on what it knows instead of on what it thinks'. But, as if to illustrate the contradiction at the heart of the venture, Scott himself had said, 'The Southern Journey involves the most important object of the Expedition.' In the end, reconciling this conflict proved beyond the reach of both practical planning and human endurance.

The Worst Journey in the World then edges towards an even more unacceptable conclusion – that the jingoism and heroic amateurism in which the nation took such pride had been a weakness rather than a strength. Going further, and despite his own archaic opinions on so many other issues, Cherry argued for a more modern approach to major scientific endeavour –

'These things cannot be done by individual heroes and enthusiasts cadging for cheques from rich men and grants from private scientific societies: it is a business ... for public organisation.'

Most controversially of all, *The Worst Journey in the World* departed from Edwardian traditions of deferential, almost hagiographical, writing about the Empire's heroes by venturing on criticism of Scott himself. While acknowledging the expedition leader's courage and powers of endurance, and paying tribute to the love and loyalty he had commanded, Cherry made it clear that, in his view, it was weak planning that had led to the deaths of Wilson and the others.

&

Any story of the British Antarctic Expedition must, sooner or later, consider the long shadow of the Norwegian Roald Amundsen. Yes, it was a serious scientific exploration, not a race to be first to the Pole. But of course it hurt that, after such a journey, Amundsen had beaten them to it.

In the responses of Scott's men, and in Cherry's own writings, there is more than a trace of resentment – a scarce-hidden suggestion that Amundsen had not quite 'played the game'. To begin with, he had set out from Christiana announcing that he was bound for the North Pole, his true destination known only to his brother. When, on leaving Madeira, he had suddenly declared that he was heading south, Scott and his team had been outraged at the deception. Voyaging to the Antarctic in the *Fram*, a ship specially designed for coping with pack-ice, the Norwegians had also had the temerity to disembark at the closest point, a mere seventy miles from the Pole. From their base at the Bay of Whales, Amundsen's teams of over a hundred Greenland dogs then easily outstripped Scott's motley collection of clapped-out Siberian ponies (all of which were worked to death before being eaten by both dogs and men). Besides, weren't Norwegians practically born on skis? Worst of all, Amundsen hadn't spent months travelling to and fro collecting specimens and taking scientific measurements. He had merely dashed to the Pole and back. It was 'a feat', but it wasn't really exploration. Damn it, the man hadn't even brought back any penguins' eggs.

It was Shaw who muted this voice. 'I said to Cherry one day,' wrote the great man, 'that international courtesy and sportsmanship made it advisable to be scrupulously just and polite to Amundsen. I suspect that this was the hardest pill for him to swallow; for the moment that he went into the question he had to admit that Amundsen was no scallawag, but a very great explorer'. In this and much else, Shaw's wisdom seems to have sobered Cherry's intemperance.

It was, by any standards, an unlikely collaboration. Two more different characters than George Bernard Shaw and Apsley Cherry-Garrard would be hard to imagine: Shaw the international Socialist and proto-feminist; Cherry-Garrard the suffragette-hating Tory imperialist; Shaw who despised the idle rich and especially landowners who lived off the rents of the poor; Cherry-Garrard who collected his rents and looked down on the working classes and their appalling trade unions. Even in artistic matters, the two were opposites: Shaw the first of the truly modern British playwrights; Cherry-Garrard who thought modern art was a 'malaise of the mind' and preferred Old Masters like Velasquez' *The Rokeby Venus* to which a suffragette had recently applied an axe.

Yet through the accident of being neighbours, the two became friends. And *The Worst Journey in the World* was the beneficiary. So much so that Cherry was anxious to acknowledge his debt to Shaw in print. The older man would have none of it, arguing that the sum total of his relevant experience was the great frost of 1878 when he had skated on the Serpentine in Hyde Park. Yet without Shaw, Cherry might have allowed his own prejudices and resentments to burn more brightly. And *The Worst Journey in the World* would have been the poorer for it.

The book restored Cherry's reputation and brought him a certain celebrity. But it did not save him. Drifting deeper into depression, he became ever more crusty and querulous, falling out with everybody, including Scott's widow. Occasionally doing a little bird watching, he sat day after day in his summer house at Lamer Park, every so often winding the handle that rotated the platform under his chair to vary the view.

With his lifelong love of open spaces, it is surprising that Cherry-Garrard chose to live the last decades of his life in London instead of at the house he had planned to build below the Wittenham Clumps. Perhaps his obsession with Antarctic memories, with lost friends and old grievances, made the distractions of London more valuable to him than the peace and quiet of Wittenham Wood. Perhaps, also, the Antarctic years had left him with a kind of frostbite of the mind; perhaps, looking up at the twin hills of the Wittenham Clumps he would have seen the twin volcanoes of Mount Erebus and Mount Terror that had dominated the view from the expedition's base camp; perhaps, sitting on his veranda overlooking the gentle Thames he would have seen only the Beardsmore Glacier where Titus Oates had so bravely given up his life; maybe, fishing from his landing stage, he would have remembered the time they had killed a seal and, opening it up, been delighted to find thirty-six fish that were only half-digested and still edible.

Gradually he lost interest in his estates. The Little Wittenham project was abandoned. The Manor House and the Wittenham Clumps were sold off, as was Lamer Park. At one point, his land agent had suggested that he might like to donate part of his Little Wittenham estate, possibly including the Clumps with their Iron Age hill fort, to the National Trust. Cherry-Garrard refused, commenting that even King Charles had not been expected to pay his executioners. Eventually, taxes and poor health forced him to sell off his other properties and confine himself to his London flat where he spent the last thirteen years of his life collecting books, complaining about the noise, drinking strong coffee, quarrelling with neighbours and sitting in the bay window of his library leafing through his Antarctic journals.

✌✢

For all the later years of obsession and depression, it is impossible to believe that Cherry-Garrard regretted answering the call of the Antarctic. That it left him with enduring mental and physical scars is certain. But it also left him with an enduring admiration for the men with whom he had journeyed, and a conviction that the true meaning of the expedition was not the conquest of the Pole or even the furtherance of science, but what he called 'the response of the spirit'. *The Worst Journey in the World* is not a boastful book, but the pride that does show through is not so much pride in overcoming the ordeal of Cape Crozier, but in the way he, Bowers and Wilson had conducted themselves in the teeth of almost certain death. Often that spirit came down to apparently trivial things, like 'not forgetting the Please and Thank You, which means much in such circumstances'.

And at the centre of it all was the man whose character made him, in Cherry's eyes, the true hero of the expedition. Edward Adrian Wilson, known to them all as 'Uncle Bill', had led Cherry and Bowers on 'the worst journey'. And it was on that expedition that the man whom Cherry had described as 'pure gold' had shown his mettle. He was not alone in believing that Wilson was special. Scott also wrote: 'Words must always fail when I talk of him. I believe he is the finest character I ever met – the closer one gets to him the more there is to admire. Every quality is so solid and dependable. Whatever the matter, one knows Bill will be sound, shrewdly practical, intensely loyal, and quite unselfish.'

It was this last quality, the unselfishness of the man, which made such a deep impression on Cherry-Garrard. 'If I were asked what was the greatest of Wilson's many qualities,' he wrote, 'I would reply that he was a man who never for one moment thought of himself.' 'Wilson's idea,' he said in his final tribute, 'was forgetfulness of self. By putting that idea into action as well as in contemplation, and in suffering ... he had reached another plateau which is round no earthly Pole, where he was beyond ambition and beyond fear. He had the quiet mind.'

In this, Wilson came to embody all of Cherry's own unrealised ideals. For in journeying away from self-preoccupation, Wilson had made the journey that mattered. And in doing so had found the Pole of the quiet mind that monks and mystics through the ages have referred to as the *quies*. It was the test that Cherry himself could not pass, the journey he could not make, the quiet he could not find. And his tragedy, he knew, was that he had failed in this, the greatest expedition of all.

'The happiest days of my life' – Apsley Cherry-Garrard, who inherited the estate and Manor of Little Wittenham and undertook 'The worst journey in the world' *(photograph: Herbert Ponting)*

'The finest character I ever met' – Dr Edward Wilson *(photograph: Edward Thomas Wilson)*

The Worst Journey In The World, by Apsley Cherry-Garrard, and Sara Wheeler's superb biography – *Cherry: A Life of Apsley Cherry-Garrard* – are both available from Vintage / Penguin Random House.

Captain Robert Scott's diary, including his harrowing record of the journey back from the South Pole, is available to read in the Virtual Books section of the British Library website.

3

A Frail Grip on the Earth

I have passed these trees here on the Clumps a hundred times and more without ever giving them either thought or thanks. Yet reaching out a hand to touch the fine trunk of this mature beech tree, feeling its quiet presence and solidity, it suddenly seems obvious that trees like this have given us ... nearly everything. Most of the oxygen we breathe. All of the coal on which our modern world was built. The paper we write and print on. And for most of our history trees like this have given us shelter and shade, homes and roofs, floors and furniture, doors and beams, fuel and firewood, carts and carriages, boats and bridges, churches and barns, fences and tools, bows and arrows, corks and barrels, nuts and fruits, and a thousand other products from tannins for curing leather to galls, inks, and charcoals for our first writings and cellulose for our LCD screens.

In the case of the oak tree, it was the nutritious, plentiful, and storable acorn that was probably our first staple. In maturity, oaks were 'England's wooden walls' – giving us the ships of Drake and Nelson. In the case of the beech tree, it was the smooth, pale, delicate bark that gave us the material on which many of Europe's earliest records were written. It is even possible that 'book' is derived from ancient words for the beech tree, including *boc* in Old English, *buche* in German, and *beuk* in Dutch – which may be why students in mediaeval times sometimes wore a square of beech bark as a badge of learning. Of more practical use to mediaeval villagers, it was beech leaves that filled a million early mattresses, being particularly favoured in France where the rustling of the leaves earned them the name *lits de parlement* – 'talking beds'.

From bodily comforts to spiritual matters, the Celts who built these great earthworks here on the Clumps believed that the beech gave their Druid priests the power to get in touch with the ancestors and access the wisdom of the ages. More than two millennia later, equally interesting claims were being made by a local doctor, Edward Bach, who developed his famous system of flower remedies in the village of Brightwell-cum-Sotwell, just below the Wittenham Clumps. Bach's home and flower garden are today a place of homeopathic pilgrimage, where a beech flower tincture is still recommended for people who are in what Bach called the 'beech state'. Apparently, the symptoms of this malady are 'lack of compassion and understanding of the circumstances and paths that other people are given,' leading to 'intolerance of difference' and 'outbursts of irritability.' The remedy for this is to transfer the energy of beech flowers by floating them in pure water for three hours in direct sunlight. The flower-powered water is then mixed with an equal amount of brandy to make the mother tincture, which must then be diluted further by mixing two drops with another thirty millilitres of brandy. The result is particularly effective, perhaps not altogether surprisingly, for those who 'feel the need to see more good and beauty in all that surrounds them.'

Cataloguing all these properties and uses cannot of course capture the delight that the beech tree gives in its own right: in its graceful grey limbs soaring like cathedral arches to the stained-glass canopy above; in the two-day miracle of its unfurling green freshness in the spring; in the filtered sunlight dappling last year's leaves on the forest floor; in the spectacular delicacy of bluebells blooming quietly in the shade of a beech wood.

All this no doubt inspired the artist Paul Nash who painted the Wittenham beeches so many times over the years (Chapter *No glimmer of God's hand*). But to Nash, trees seemed to offer something beyond aesthetic pleasure. 'I know they are people,' he wrote, 'wonderfully beautiful people.'

For a more measured insight into what people and beech trees might have in common, we had better turn to the German ecologist, Peter Wohlleben, who compares beech trees to humans in the way they 'bring up' their children. Mature trees, he explains, prevent their saplings from growing up too fast by controlling how much light they allow through the leaf canopy. Restricting the rate of growth in this way ensures that the cells of the young trees are small and densely packed, making the wood stronger, more flexible, and less susceptible to wind damage or fungal rot. By the miracle of evolution, it is as if the tree has always known what science has only recently discovered – that the slow growth of a beech sapling in the early years improves the odds of a long and healthy life. And all the while, these same beech trees are using their underground root systems to supplement the sugars and nutrients that the saplings are able to draw from the soil (Chapter *The Sermon on the Clumps*). All this, says Wohlleben, is why the term 'upbringing' has long been used by foresters to describe the relationship of beech trees to the rising generation.

For a more superficial parallel, a wander around the beeches of the Wittenham Clumps also reveals that the trunks are slim and smooth-barked in youth, put on weight and girth in middle age, develop wrinkles in later life, and attempt to cover up the lines and creases with 'make-up' of moss or crustose lichen. Indeed, it is apparently possible to make a rough estimate of the age of a beech tree by how much mossy make-up it uses.

More seriously, the wonderfully variegated beech leaves in autumn – sharp green, lemon yellow, bitter orange and old gold – are also the signs of the tree setting humans an example by undertaking an annual detox regime to get fit and ready for the winter. As Richard Mabey puts it:

> … leaf-fall provides an opportunity for the tree to get rid of waste products built up over the year, including toxins absorbed from the soil … At the same time, the tree is breaking down the chlorophyll and sugars in its leaves and withdrawing them into its woody parts, conserving them. When the green goes, what is left are the brightly coloured carotenoids – orange and brown and yellow antioxidant chemicals similar to those that make tomatoes red – which are believed to bind with the toxins. This flurry of chemical activity is stressful for the leaves, and to protect them during the crucial transfer of chlorophyll many trees synthesise yet another antioxidant, the bright red antho-cyanin … That is what the season of mellow fruitfulness is all about. The time of high colouring isn't a signal of fading away, but of detox vitality, ruddiness, rude health.

Returning to these particular beeches here on the Wittenham Clumps, it seems that they were planted sometime in the early 1740s, soon to be followed by places like Chanctonbury Ring on the Sussex Downs and by the clumps to be found in the grounds of stately homes like Blenheim Palace. Strange, then, to think that hill-top beech clumps – so much admired, photographed and enjoyed by visitors today – were once the centre of a great controversy.

It was in the eighteenth century that philosophical arguments about the nature of beauty began to occupy the minds of the otherwise unemployed. Until then, the accepted view had been that raw nature had the potential to be beautiful, but that human intervention was needed for that potential to be realised.

'The living landscape,' wrote the novelist Horace Walpole – son of Britain's first Prime Minister – must be 'chastened or polished.' Improving on nature was therefore the order of the day. And the go-to man for the job was Walpole's friend Lancelot Brown, known to history as 'Capability Brown' from his habit of always telling potential clients that their grounds had the 'capability' of being improved.

Capability Brown, fifth child of a land agent and a chambermaid, improved more than a hundred and seventy gardens and parks in England – adding a few trees here, felling a few there, and perhaps suggesting a ha-ha or an artificial lake (with the option of planting a fast-growing copse of evergreens to screen off the unsightly dwellings of the poor). But where an additional tree or two was required to complete the effect, there was an obvious problem: rich clients couldn't be expected to wait thirty or forty years to enjoy what they had paid for. Brown's solution was the 'transplanting engine'.

The process began with the digging of a trench around a mature beech tree. This was then filled with manure to encourage the growth of capillary roots close to the surface. As we shall see, these fine, complex, tendril-like root systems are conveniently shallow, often penetrating only a few inches into the earth. They nonetheless do the bulk of the work in providing the tree with its moisture and nutrients. Once the roots had begun to establish themselves, teams of men worked them up out of the soil with a light pickaxe, known as the 'tree picker'. The heavy work came next, levering under the root system, working first one side and then the other, until the tree could be leaned and lowered, roots and all, on to the transplanting engine. This was little more than two large iron wheels on either side of a strong central pole onto which the tree was lashed. Everything secured, two 'balance men' placed themselves at strategic points astride the trunk to keep it level while oxen or carthorses hauled it off to its new home.

Brown's work is often dismissed by modern landscape gardeners. But even in Brown's day, the idea of 'improving' had its critics. The poet Richard Owen Cambridge said that he hoped to die before Brown so that he could see heaven before it was improved. And towards the end of the century, the picturesque movement began to put forward the argument that real beauty resided in the very lack of perfection and polish that Capability Brown was striving to achieve. 'What is more beautiful,' wrote William Gilpin, 'than an old tree with a hollow trunk? or with a dead arm, a drooping bough, or a dying branch?'

And it was the beech clump – that signature feature of a Capability Brown landscape – that came in for particular contempt. Sir Uvedale Price, another leading advocate of the picturesque, and author of the 1794 'Essay on the Picturesque, As Compared with the Sublime and the Beautiful,' wrote:

> The great distinguishing feature of modern improvement is the clump – a name, which if the first letter were taken away, would most accurately describe its form and effect. Were it made the object of study how to invent something, which, under the name of ornament, should disfigure whole districts, nothing could be contrived to answer that purpose like a clump. Natural groups, being formed by trees of different ages and sizes, and at different distances from each other, often too by a mixture of those of the largest size, with thorns, hollies, and others of inferior growth, are full of variety in their outlines. And from the same causes, no two groups are exactly alike. But clumps, from the trees being generally of the same age and growth, from their being planted nearly at the same distance in a circular form, and from each tree being equally pressed by his neighbour, are as like each other as so many puddings turned out of one common mould.

Price, who fretted that the French Revolution would spread to his estates in Hertfordshire, also objected to Capability Brown's landscaping on the grounds that it embodied 'solitary grandeur and power', and so served to emphasise the alienation between landowner and worker. Richard Payne Knight MP – another leading light of the picturesque and expert on phallic imagery – was more sympathetic to what was happening across the Channel and argued that 'improvement' was suppressing nature and therefore a symbol of the oppression of suffering humanity. By way of this reasoning, he urged the poor to rise up and vandalise Brown's celebrated parks and gardens.

Through such controversies, the seemingly innocent act of planting clumps of trees came to be seen almost as an act of aggression in a class war. Indeed just such a claim had been made in the previous century by the agriculturalist John Houghton, who argued that the point of planting trees in conspicuous places was that 'they make or preserve a grandeur, and cause them to be respected by their poorer neighbours.' Capability Brown's successor as 'England's greatest gardener', Humphry Repton, made the point even more bluntly by acknowledging that his work was intended to achieve, 'that charm which only belongs to ownership, the exclusive right of enjoyment, with the power of refusing that others should share our pleasure.' (This may seem like the long-gone snobbery of a bygone age, but it still has echoes today in the many new houses that are described by estate agents as 'an exclusive development'.)

On the other hand, we can make too much out of the great clumps controversy. It may be true, as Richard Mabey says, that Capability Brown's hill-top tree clumps were 'a ritual display of power over the land, a visible demonstration of status'. But they may also represent what seems to be a natural temptation to place something to mark the top of a dome, whether a tree on a hill, a flag on a sandcastle, a bobble on a woolly hat, or a cherry on a cupcake.

❧❧

At the same time as Brown and his contemporaries were arguing over the merits of transplanting a tree here or planting a clump there, vast acreages of Britain's woodlands were falling to the saw and the axe in the cause of both the agricultural revolution and the navy's need for ships-of-the-line. For the most part, beech woods were spared the worst of this carnage. As in the Chilterns, the beech tends to be found on thin soils and on the slopes of chalk downs, neither well-suited to the new agriculture. Nor was beech of much use for shipbuilding. Even the demand for bright-burning beech firewood was diminishing as the railways began to make coal available almost everywhere, replacing beech wood in local industries like the Henley glassworks.

So it was the oak woods that suffered the deepest cuts. And it was the beech that took advantage of the open spaces left behind. As a consequence, our chalk downlands gradually became more and more the domain of the beech trees that are the glory of the Chilterns today.

But even more than the centuries of shipbuilding and Enclosure Acts, it was the second half of the twentieth century that devastated Britain's trees. In the three decades after 1950, as much as half of the country's ancient woodland was lost to agriculture and commercial forms of forestry in what Mabey describes as 'an act of collective vandalism that has no parallel in our landscape history.' To cite one example, the oaks of Stanstead Great Wood in Suffolk were cleared using a component of Agent Orange, the chemical used by the United States to deforest large areas of Vietnam. At one point, even the National Trust joined in, felling mature beeches on its Ashridge Estate in the Chilterns and replanting them with conifers. It was in these years, also, that an estimated one hundred and forty thousand miles of Britain's hedgerows were uprooted to make way for ever-larger farm machines.

Once again, the beech woods managed to escape the worst. But their turn was coming. And it arrived at two o'clock in the morning of October 16th, 1987. For more than four hours that night, winds of one hundred miles an hour tore through the south-east of England, killing eighteen people, bringing down power and telephone lines, blocking roads and railways, wrecking gardens and parks – and ripping fifteen million trees from the ground. Across the Channel, twice as many trees were lost as the winds swept a twenty-five-mile corridor across Normandy and Brittany virtually clear of woods. All across the chalklands of Hampshire, the South Downs, Sussex and the Kentish Weald, beech trees of all ages were torn from the earth. In the Chilterns, the winds that funnelled up through the folds and valleys brought down whole swathes of beech trees like helpless infantry cut down by a hail of fire. Above Ewelme and across from Swyncombe to Britwell Hill, the woods were littered with downed trees, their root-plates standing on edge so that it was possible to see how spectacularly fine and shallow those roots really were. And gripped in their thousand frail fingers were the fragments of white chalk and dark clots of soil that showed how desperately they had tried to cling on to the earth that night.

As for the hill-top beech clumps, some like these here at Wittenham were left punch-drunk but still standing. Others, like the clump on Chanctonbury Ring on the South Downs lost three-quarters of their trees.

༄༅

In the aftermath of the Great Storm, two important lessons were learnt about our beech woods. The first was that they have far greater powers of self-regeneration than had been imagined. All the heroic efforts at replanting by the National Trust, and other conservation authorities, were of small effect compared with the response of the beech woods themselves. In the empty and suddenly light-filled glades, where so many millions of trees had gone down, even greater numbers of seeds and saplings seized their chance. So much so that the beech glades of the Chilterns are today almost as magnificent as ever.

The second and more worrying truth to emerge was that the Great Storm of 1987 had not acted alone. Its accomplice was the drought of a dozen years earlier that had so damaged the root systems of the beech trees that they were unable to hold on in the hurricane-force winds that swept through on that October night. The great evolved advantage of beech trees – the frail, spidery, close-to-the-surface root system that had enabled them to thrive on thin, chalky soils – had now proved their downfall. Those root systems are often as little as half a metre deep, but, spreading wide and shallow, they can draw enough moisture and nutrients from the thinnest of soils. It is an evolutionary strategy marvellously well adapted to England's climate. But come drought or sustained warmer temperatures, and strength turns to weakness as the top layers of soil dry out, leaving beech roots drawing on dust and struggling to maintain their frail grip on the earth.

And now we have arrived at the real fear for the future of the beech in England. Because of this special susceptibility to drought or warmer temperatures, it is perhaps the most vulnerable of all our trees in an era of climate change. 'As our climate continues to warm,' says Alistair Jump, Professor of Biological and Environmental Sciences at Stirling University, 'droughts will become more frequent and more extreme ... Beech forests across Europe will be hit increasingly hard, with a high risk of widespread mortality when the next big dry spell hits, particularly in southern parts of the UK.'

How quickly this might happen is difficult to predict. The Sylva Foundation, located here below the Clumps in the village of Long Wittenham, is one of Britain's leading woodlands research centres. Its founder and CEO, Gabriel Hemery, says that on current best-estimates it will take perhaps fifty or sixty years for the climate of Oxfordshire to become similar to that of the South of France today. If that happens, then, among many other changes to our countryside, the beech tree is likely to disappear.

In the case of the Wittenham Clumps, the signs of ill health are already evident, though whether this has to do with climate change cannot yet be known. The Earth Trust, which owns the Clumps, has long been trying to preserve the beeches on both Round and Fort Hills. But faced with global heating, it has been decided that some of the trees being planted to maintain the Wittenham Clumps should be not beech but hornbeam and small-leaved lime. The same conclusion has been reached by the National Trust in its concern to protect another famous stand of beech on the Kingston Lacey Estate in Dorset. The Estate's eccentric nineteenth-century owner planted three hundred and sixty-five beech trees on one side of the drive, one for each day of the year, and three hundred and sixty-six on the other side, to accommodate the leap year. Those trees are now nearing the end of their lives and the Trust has decided to replant. But not with beech. Given both air pollution and climate change, it has reluctantly been decided that the beech is not a good long-term bet. Instead, hornbeams have been planted alongside the existing beech avenue and will eventually replace it.

It is a bitter twist to this story that the trees that have given us so many benefits over the centuries have also given us climate change: there are other contributors to the rise in atmospheric CO_2 in our times, but a major culprit has been the Age of Coal that has burned the carbon from billions of prehistoric trees. The proposed solutions, as we know, range from carbon taxes to climate engineering. But it is also possible that part of the solution might come from trees themselves. According to a report featured in *The Guardian* in 2019, the planting of billions of trees could potentially remove about two-thirds of the additional CO_2 that human activity has put into the atmosphere. 'It isn't just one of our climate change solutions,' says the report's author, 'it is overwhelmingly the top one.' In 2019, political parties in the UK seemed to warm to the idea, with Labour promising to plant four billion trees by 2040, and the Conservatives a more modest thirty million more trees a year. The Green Party, meanwhile, offered seven hundred million by 2030.

Other countries have made similar promises. But even if it were to become an international reality, mass tree planting might take a century to do the job of removing a significant amount of the CO_2 that we have put into the atmosphere. By that time, it may be too late for the planet. Almost certainly it will be too late for the beech trees here on the Wittenham Clumps and across the downlands of southern England. 'In the not too distant future,' says Richard Mabey in his wonderful book *The Ash and the Beech* from which much of the information in this essay is drawn, 'beech trees are likely to exist only in photographs and in our memories.'

4

A Roman road to reality

The view from the Wittenham Clumps encompasses many picturesque Oxfordshire villages – Little Wittenham, Dorchester-on-Thames, Clifton Hampden, Aston Tirrold, Brightwell-cum-Sotwell – with their listed manor houses, thatched cottages and eye-watering property prices. And then there is Berinsfield.

Plans put forward in the 1960s for two high-rise apartment blocks came to nothing, and so it is the concrete water tower poking up just to the north of Dorchester's mellow and ancient abbey, that identifies Berinsfield in the view from the north-east side of the Clumps.

I first heard the name of Berinsfield when I was a student a few miles down the road at Wadham College. To this day, the Oxford colleges preserve a Downton Abbey era system of college servants, or 'Scouts', typically one for each staircase. The Scout for my rooms was a formidable character called Billy, six-foot-something with dyed blond hair and a taste for traditional Town vs. Gown brawling at Carfax of a Saturday evening. He also had a side-line as an unofficial debt collector, an occupation which seemed to involve frequent turning over of hot-dog vans on Oxford's High Street. Billy lived in Berinsfield, and it was from him that I first learned of its existence. But even without the benefit of the local colour Billy provided, most people who lived in South Oxfordshire at the time knew Berinsfield as a 'problem estate'.

Unsurprisingly, then, residents of Berinsfield have sometimes felt looked down upon from the heights of greater affluence around them. Forty years ago, for example, an issue of the Berinsfield newsletter was devoted to the theme of 'Us against those who would try to put us down.' The issue attracted the attention of Radio Oxford who sent reporter Richard Stanley to interview residents. 'Many of the critics,' said one, 'have never visited our village.'

On the other hand, unless you live in Berinsfield there is little reason to visit. It is not known for its gastropubs or historic churches. Nor is it on the way to anywhere. By-passed and cut off by the main Oxford to Henley road, it remains unknown even to many who have lived nearby all their lives.

I too had never visited Berinsfield. And that might still be the case if, one morning, I had not extended my walk from the Wittenham Clumps – crossing the Thames at Day's Lock and attempting to follow the route of the old Roman road through Dorchester to the Baldons. Clearly marked on the map, the road once travelled by the legions now leads straight through the middle of the estate.

The short walk via Lay Avenue and Evenlode Drive was enough to blow away some of the cobwebs of prejudice that had clung to me as I had brushed against them over the years. I had heard the stories and had perhaps half expected to see damp plywood at the windows and gardens full of weeds and old prams. On leaving via the old Roman road that heads out across open fields, I felt ashamed of myself. Most of Berinsfield's homes and gardens have as much pride taken in them as houses anywhere else.

On returning home, I set Google on the case and a few minutes later had assembled the following facts, courtesy of the *Oxford City Council and District Data Service.*

- The employment rate in Berinsfield is higher than the national average.
- The proportion of people claiming Jobseekers Allowance or Universal Credit is lower than the national average.

- The percentage of sixteen-to-twenty-four-year-olds on benefits is less than half the national average.
- The crime rate, both for 'all crimes' and 'violent crimes', is less than half the national average.
- The home ownership rate is higher than the national average.
- The rate of binge drinking is lower than the average for both Oxfordshire and England as a whole.
- The proportion of people in Berinsfield who have 'given unpaid help at least once a month in the last year' is over thirty per cent (national average twenty-three per cent).

My morning walk had, I found, led me to a somewhat uncomfortable conclusion. In many ways, Berinsfield does indeed offer a contrast to its surrounding towns and villages. The average house price in 2020, for example, was £240,000, whereas two miles up the road in Dorchester-on-Thames it was £630,000. But as these few facts show, Berinsfield does not offer a contrast to the nation as a whole: by most socio-economic measures it performs considerably better than the all-England average.

I did not grow up within sight of the Wittenham Clumps; my youth was spent in a back-to-back terrace house in the cobbled streets of a northern industrial city. Because of this, I had fondly imagined that I had a reasonably realistic idea of life in Britain as a whole. But living in different villages of south Oxfordshire for more than forty years had taken its toll. And my walk on the old Roman road that day led me to a realisation, or at least to a reminder, of what I should have known: it is Berinsfield that much more closely represents life in Britain today than Little Wittenham, Dorchester-on-Thames, Aston Tirrold, Clifton Hampden, or Brightwell-cum-Sotwell.

☙❧

The other obvious contrast between Berinsfield and many of the surrounding villages is that it dates not from the Middle Ages but from the 1960s. Yet its history is arguably more interesting than the annals of many more ancient hamlets.

That history begins with World War II when what is now Berinsfield was a bleak, wind-blown airstrip known as Mount Farm. Once the grass of its runways had been replaced by hard standing, it became one of the bases from which Wellingtons and Lysanders took to the skies to join the controversial heavy bomber raids that destroyed cities like Cologne and Dresden. It was when returning from one such mission, on the night of July 7th, 1941, that a twenty-two-year-old New Zealander crawled out along the wing of his Wellington bomber to put out an engine fire. For his extraordinary courage, Sergeant James Ward was awarded the Victoria Cross. Two months later, he was killed in a night raid over Hamburg.

By 1943, intelligence gleaned from aerial photography had become key to the Allied push for victory, and it was at this time that Mount Farm became the base of the Seventh Photographic Reconnaissance Group of the United States Eighth Army Air Force commanded by Lieutenant Colonel Elliott Roosevelt, son of the American President.

It was unusual for the US Airforce to ask help from the RAF, but Mount Farm had the task of being 'the eyes of the Eighth' and Colonel Roosevelt was shrewd enough to request the services of Squadron Leader Adrian Warburton. Twice awarded the Distinguished Service Order and twice the Distinguished Flying Cross, Warburton 'flew every bomber like a fighter', bringing down nine enemy aircraft. In completing more than four hundred reconnaissance missions over enemy territory, he helped provide priceless intelligence in the build-up to the Allied invasion of Europe but did not live to see its success. On the morning of April 12th, 1944, he took off from Mount Farm in a Lockheed Lightning on a mission to

'The eyes of the eighth' – A strip of broken and overgrown concrete on the edge of Berinsfield is now all that remains of the Mount Farm airfield that played a vital role in the build-up to the Allied invasion of Europe in June, 1944.

photograph targets in Nazi Germany. He was never seen again.

Meanwhile, true to their reputation, the Americans were bringing a touch of Hollywood to the place that was soon to become Berinsfield. Stars like Dorothy Lamour, Bing Crosby and Bob Hope all performed in Mount Farm's giant blister hangers. And it was here, too, that Glenn Miller gave his last performance before flying off to entertain US troops in Paris, disappearing somewhere over the channel in what became one of the great romantic mysteries of the war.

≈≈

Any glamour there might have been disappeared in 1945 when the Dakotas headed back to their home base in Colorado Springs, leaving behind a collection of drab wooden huts and weed-strewn runways in the middle of an exhausted and almost bankrupt country.

Within months, the destitute of war, the homeless and the bombed-out had begun to move in.

Usually without running water, toilets or kitchens, the abandoned huts were unsuitable as family homes. Yet in the housing crisis of the post-war years, ex-military camps and Nissen huts put a roof over the heads of thousands. Some of the homeless were encouraged to move in by desperate local councils. Others didn't wait to be asked. By late 1946 there were over a thousand ex-military squatter camps across Britain in which forty thousand people were attempting to rebuild their lives. One of them was Oxfordshire's Mount Farm airbase.

Judging by the old photographs, it was a miserable-looking place of weeds and washing lines, of huts clad in wood or felt, of standpipes and Elsan sanitation buckets, of underweight children and overworked parents. But it was home and neighbourhood to more than one hundred and fifty families, all of them living on a promise that they would be rehoused within twelve months. Fourteen years later, most were still there. One couple, Joan and Kermit Bateman, had twelve children while they waited.

Funds for re-housing were finally approved in the late 1950s by a Council 'conscious of the squalor in which many of the hut dwellers were living'. Unusually, re-housing did not mean moving people out. Instead, a new village was to be built on the existing site. That site, like so much of Oxfordshire's land, belonged to an Oxford college – in this case Corpus Christi – and was bought by the Council for £128 per acre.

To lay out what was enthusiastically described as 'the first new village to be built in England for over two hundred years' the Council employed Sir William Holford, later to become the first town planner to be elevated to the House of Lords. Perhaps better known for his work at Eton College, Sir William visited the Mount Farm site and, though noting that it departed from good planning practice by being a long way from any source of employment, declared that he 'couldn't see a reason why it wouldn't succeed'.

Initially, there were to be two hundred and seventy-eight 'modern homes with spacious gardens at back and front', and all were to be finished with 'Tyrolean' – a light coloured render. Most were to be rented, though about sixty were put on sale at £1,000 each with the idea that losses on rent arrears could be offset by profits from sales. All of the dwellings were to have grassed open fronts – leading early residents to complain that children were always coming to stand at the front windows to see what was happening in other people's living rooms. Planting hedges for privacy was not allowed, as they might become untidy, and the mowing of the front lawns was to be the responsibility of the Council, not the tenant. This was described by the Council as 'finding a balance between paternalism and laissez-faire.'

In order to leave behind the associations of the Mount Farm camp, the new model village was also to have a new name. Suggestions included Wimblestraw, Lynchwell, Biborough, Cropwell and Shadwell. Eventually, the local Catholic priest suggested a combination of the old and the new: 'Berin', after the local Saint Birinus, or Berin, who had converted this part of Wessex to Christianity in the seventh century, and 'The Field', which was the name the Americans aircrews had given to the camp. Berinsfield was born. And to show that the spirit of enterprise had survived, some of the families began breaking up the eighteen-inch thick concrete of the old runways to sell to the Council as hardcore.

Naming the streets and avenues should have been a simpler affair, but it was not without problems. One street was due to be named Holford Avenue, after the planner, but Sir William declared that he would not have his name put to any part of the village after what the local council had done to his original plan. Bullingdon Rural District Council, in a flash of inspiration, named it Bullingdon Avenue.

Whether the fault of council or planner, the 'new model village' soon came in for criticism. Lionel Brett in '*Landscape in Decline*' wrote that 'Something went wrong. The 'village' is no such thing but just another council estate.' Architectural historian Jennifer Sherwood described it as 'a missed opportunity, with brick semis and terraces of the most dismal kind, sprawled out aimlessly along dreary streets'.

✍

For some, including many of the new residents, the problem was not the houses but the people to whom they were being allocated. It is not known how many sociologists it takes to calculate that if you take all the 'problem families' and put them into the same estate then you will likely end up with a 'problem estate'. But something of the kind seems to have been what happened in Berinsfield, and by the mid-1960s, the model village was already being referred to as 'Dodge City'.

Fortunately, two Oxford sociologists took a less superficial interest and began interviewing residents to find out what they thought about their new model village.[4] Initially, they reported, there was 'widespread excitement and pride occasioned by living in a new house after the experience of a hut or of life with in-laws'. One tenant is quoted as saying that her ten-year-old son was 'so thrilled that he insists on getting in the bath every single day'. Another commented that many families were taking 'a new pride in themselves and their appearance'. One noted that 'The majority have ... got cleaner and tidier ... some had lost interest in life altogether, but they've bucked up now – it lifts them up in themselves.' Some even felt intimidated by the change – 'You're always worried about the house and frightened of the children touching anything.' The Oxford Mail also interviewed some of the newly installed residents one of whom, a Mrs Deak, told the reporter 'I'm happier here than I've ever been'.

Not everyone was as satisfied. A new house was such a prize that the question of to whom the houses were allocated, and in what order, soon became a source of tensions. Those who had lived for many years in the huts of Mount Farm had become a community with a strong sense of identity, born of shared struggles, and they fully expected to be rehoused first. But the Council also had a waiting list of fourteen thousand 'outsider' families, and the most desperate cases began to be moved in as soon as the first streets were completed. To the Mount Farm dwellers, the incomers were queue jumpers. Some said they were being treated as just 'the scruff from the camp'. The incomers, for their part, clearly felt the resentment – 'It's only a friendly place,' said one, 'if you lived in the camp before.'

Virtually all the residents were happy to describe themselves to the researchers as working class (there was only one non-manual worker). But that didn't prevent class divisions opening up between those who thought of themselves as 'respectable' and those whom they saw as 'people who don't care how they live'. In the words of one of the 'respectable' families, 'If they wanted a model village they got the wrong people'. The sociol-ogists preferred to use the term 'unsatisfactory tenants', a category defined by 'rent arrears, neglect of house and garden, and nuisance to the community.'

With the help of the parish church, it didn't take long to find a Berinsfield resident who remembered the original Mount Farm camp. Angie Bowden, now nearing seventy, works at Bromilow's, the newsagent's, and still rises at four o'clock every morning to be at work by five. It was somewhat later than that when I met her in the nearby church hall to find that she had already brought together a collection of old press cuttings, maps, letters, photocopies of documents, and a few back issues of Berinsfield's newsletters.

I had almost expected it, but Angie's childhood memories of the camp were not of hardship or squalor. She was born in one of the abandoned huts and lived there until she was ten. 'One of the larger huts,' she told me, 'with three bedrooms, and one of the few with its own tap and a kitchen range.' Her memories of those years are of 'a small, close and friendly community where people helped each other out.' Among her most vivid childhood recollections are the 'finds' that her father brought home from his job at the gravel pits. 'Other children took acorns and bird feathers for the school nature table,' she tells me, 'we took mammoth tusks.'

Angie Burden's family was among the first to be rehoused and she has lived in Berinsfield ever since, seeing it grow from the original one hundred and fifty Mount Farm families to its present population of more than three thousand. When I asked her what she remembered most about being re-housed she had no hesitation: 'Running up and down the stairs. It was so exciting to have a house with stairs.' She, too, remembers that those who had been camp dwellers were sometimes looked down on, especially by those who had bought their homes and who 'thought they were a cut above'.

The collection of documents and clippings that Angie had prepared made frequent mention of her father, Colin Winterbourne. Over his years working for Amey's in the gravel extraction business, he had become knowledgeable about excavations and archaeology. The results of his efforts – from mammoth bones to high-quality flint tools and refined Roman pottery – can be seen today in Oxford's Pitt Rivers and Ashmolean Museums. 'Amey's didn't like it,' Angie remembered. 'Every time he found something important the work had to stop.'

Later, reading through Angie's papers, it became clear that Berinsfield has been served by many outstanding residents who have helped to build a strong community in the face of difficulties unfamiliar to many of its neighbouring villages. 'The place has had its ups and downs,' said Angie, 'but it's been a good place to live. I've never wanted to leave.'

5

A LAYER OF WOOLLEN AIR

It was when circling the top of Round Hill early one morning that I noticed what I took to be litter caught up in brambles. Idly thinking I should pick it up, I sat for a while on the memorial bench at the top of the grassy track that heads steeply down to Little Wittenham. As I stood to continue my walk, my eye was drawn again to the crumpled paper in what appeared to be a plastic bag at the edge of the trees. I approached and saw that it was not litter at all, but cellophane swathing half a dozen flowers – freesias – with a note.

I slipped off the elastic band and smoothed out the note. This is what it said (some words omitted to avoid revealing the identity of the writer).

> *To Dad,*
> *I know that you have been looking down on me for this past year but it doesn't feel the same without you … You're my Dad and always will be, and I love you so dearly. Please watch from above when I open my exam results.*
> *I miss you Dad.*
> *(Name omitted)*

Later in my walk, dry-eyed again, I wondered why the note and flowers had been placed in that particular spot. Had it perhaps been the scene of family picnics or a favourite walk? Or was it because the tops of hills, with their wide horizons and sense of remove, have always suggested themselves as places of significance, set apart from the world, suitable for contemplation and remembrance?

There are several other memorials to be found on the Earth Trust lands – benches donated, or trees planted in remembrance of the dead. Most are inscribed only with names and dates. On some, a few words have been added: 'who loved this spot' or 'always in our prayers.' A personal favourite is the bench in memory of Barry Dyer Lynch of Wallingford, who taught both my children at the local school. It sits in a secluded glade deep in Wittenham Woods, a spot delightful in spring for the few dozen spotted orchids growing in its broken sunlight. Another is the bench in front of Little Wittenham Parish Church, shaded by an ancient horse chestnut tree and dedicated to Len and Kathleen Barclay with an inscription that appears to be a quotation from the old man himself: 'Love your grandchildren, son and wife. Be off with ya.'

As burial loses ground to cremation, there are fewer graves and headstones to brave out the years in marble or granite. But many still feel the need for some kind of tangible reminder of a life that has gone, perhaps as a response to a sudden, inexpressible void where once there had been such vital presence. Or perhaps there is a need for memories to have some specific point around which to coalesce, as a raindrop cannot form without its speck of dust. More simply, a bench or a dedicated tree may be a place to visit for the express purpose of remembering, a space where the important takes precedence over the immediate.

But remembrance can take many different forms, and one of the many reasons for my attachment to the Wittenham Clumps is that whenever and wherever I walk on these two hills I am likely to meet with a memorial to my father in the shape of the fine teasel plants standing proud and tall on both Round and Fort Hills.

෴

From the age of thirteen to almost fifty, my father worked at Hunslet Mills, Goodman Street, in the city of Leeds. Soon after he was first made a foreman, when I suppose I must have been about five or six years old, he came home from work with a dried teasel head in his coat pocket. Warning me to handle it carefully, he explained that the scraping of its thousands of tiny, tight-packed hooks was what made the woollen blankets on my bed cosy and soft. Later, when I was old enough to be taken to the mill, he took me through the whole process of blanket making – from the arrival of bales of raw wool from Australia, to the finished article wrapped in cellophane for the department stores. After scouring came carding, spinning, weaving and milling (which cleans and thickens the cloth but leaves it matted and dense), followed by the bleaching and dyeing. Then it was on to the tentering shed (for drying the uncut cloth on 'tenterhooks') until finally we entered the raising shed where the blankets were passed several times across slowly rotating cylinders on which thousands upon thousands of the dried teasel heads were mounted so that their millions upon millions of tiny hooks could 'tease' out the fibres, raising the soft knap that I could feel whenever I touched the woollen Dodgson & Hargreaves blankets on my bed.

'A memorial to an industry …
and to a man' – Teasels on Fort Hill

Blankets have now gone the way of possers and set pots, washboards and mangles, dolly blue and washing lines across the streets, all fixtures of my childhood. Duvets do not need teasels, which even in the woollen industry have been replaced by cheaper and more durable wire brushes. But for finishing the very finest woven wools and cashmeres the teasel's combination of gentleness and strength, rigidity and elasticity, remains unsurpassed as a way of raising a knap without breaking the delicate fibres. And it is for that reason that it continues to be used by one or two manufacturers like Joshua Ellis whose mill in Batley, Yorkshire, produces fine handcrafted wool and cashmere.

Elsewhere, the long history of the teasel's usefulness in cloth making is now almost at an end. How far back that history goes is not known, but the Romans seem to have used teasels as well as bristly pig and hedgehog skins for raising a knap. In Britain, the practice goes back at least to Saxon times; the word 'teasel' seems to come from an Anglo-Saxon word, tæsel, meaning to 'tease out' fibre. Through the Middle Ages, the fuller's trade of cleaning and thickening cloth included finishing the job with teasels. 'Cloth that cometh from the weaving is nought comely to wear / Till it is fulled ... and with teasels scratched,' wrote William Langland in *Piers Plowman* in the second half of the fourteenth century. By the end of the Middle Ages, the job of the 'teaseler' had become a recognised occupation conferring entitlement to membership of the Guild of Fullers.

When Hunslet Mills began manufacturing woollen blankets in the 1920s, British production of teasels for raising cloth ran into tens of millions of plants a year. In places like Sherburn in Elmet – close to the great woollen manufacturing towns of Leeds and Wakefield, Dewsbury and Huddersfield – great armies of teasels could be seen planted in ranks and files across the fields. The phrase 'a crowd like bees in a teasel field' was apparently a common expression in the West Riding of Yorkshire, though I don't remember ever hearing it as a child.

There is even a possibility that teasels were grown commercially much closer to the Clumps, in the meadow known as 'the Hurst' that lies just across the Thames at Overy.

When those teasel farmers looked at their crops, they would have seen more than those of us who pass by the splendid teasels on the Wittenham Clumps today. They would have noted the size of the 'king' teasels at the finial to the main stalk, of the 'queens' at the end of each secondary branch, and of the 'button' thistles on the lesser outshoots, grading and pricing them according to their brittleness and ability to retain their hooked spikes under heavy use on the teasel gigs.

By my father's time, teasel production in Britain had fallen to fewer than a million heads a year. Cheaper imports from Provence and Spain had made the home-grown variety uneconomic – the same fate that finally overtook Hunslet Mills itself, which went into bankruptcy in the mid-1960s, brought low by the textile mills of Asia.

It was a sad end to a once-great industry. And also to my father's career, which over thirty-seven years had seen him rise from office boy to foreman to mill manager. His redundancy pay was a few hundred unsold woollen blankets, stacked floor-to-ceiling in our spare bedroom after my brother had left home. That summer, Dad and I tried, without much success, to sell them by knocking door-to-door along the terraces of boarding houses in Scarborough on the Yorkshire coast.

At a glance, the teasels on the Wittenham Clumps today are identical to the one my father brought home to show me that long-ago day. But a closer look would reveal a critical difference. Once the flowering is over – the palest, tenderest purple gradually giving way to the sere teasel head – what is left are the thousands of spiny flower bracts. On the wild teasel, these bracts are straight; it is only the cultivated teasel, whose bracts end in the tiny recurved hooks that make the plant suited to raising the soft knap on woven cloth.

Redundant to the textile industry the teasel may now be. But it is still vital for the goldfinches that chatter their way across the Clumps in large groups (sometimes called 'charms' from the old English 'c'irm' which described their rapid, twittering song). Alone among British birds, the goldfinch is able to push aside the spiny bracts and reach the nutritious seeds – as many as thirty thousand in a single multi-headed teasel plant. It is usually only the male goldfinch, with its narrower bill, that can manage this feat, though the females will flock to the other fine thistles that grow in glorious abundance on the banks and in the ditches of Fort Hill. In late August, I have sometimes seen a hundred or more of these sociable, colourful finches descending on a single stand of teasels or woolly thistles.

The teasel gigs are now part of industrial history (a fully operational example is kept in the Lakeland Museum in Kendal).

Arthur Adamson, second from the left, with workmates at Hunslet Mills, Leeds, in the 1930s. The photograph was taken after the men pictured had rescued a woman from drowning in the River Aire. The older man, third from right, is believed to be the mill owner. *(photograph: family collection)*

But as much as any memorial bench, the stands of teasels on the Wittenham Clumps never fail to bring my father to mind. And it was when sitting one autumn day on Fort Hill, looking at a fine stand of teasels and thinking of my father and his years amid the relentless noise of a northern textile mill, that I wrote a first draft of this poem to his memory.

Teasels

My father brought them home from Hunslet Mills
and showed me how their thousand crochet hooks
could teasel out the matted warp and weft
to raise a layer of woollen air, a final touch
to pastel perfect blankets soon to swathe
in Marks and Spencer's cellophane.
Before all this he'd seen them burst from bales
as soiled and oily wool, canvas-crushed
twelve thousand pungent miles to spring to life
in Goodman Street where he would shepherd them
from shed to shed – canal-polluting scouring
shed to carding, spinning, weaving shed where
shuttles screamed across a no-man's land of
iron looms and head-scarved women broke their
voices on the din. And then to sulphur-
stinking bleaching shed to dyeing vat to
drying shed and then on tenterhooks to
whipping shed before that final raising shed
where rattling teasel gigs scratched gentleness
from this harsh world, all the days of his life.

6

THE MAN WHO LOST AMERICA

Much of what can be seen from the twin hills of the Wittenham Clumps falls within the parish of Brightwell-cum-Sotwell. And although all of the nearby villages have featured in Britain's history, Brightwell-cum-Sotwell is, I think, the only one that can claim to have also played a significant part in the story of the United States.

The story that links this quiet village, with its many seventeenth- and eighteenth-century homes, to one of the great events of history begins in the year 1712 when Margery Bernard, wife of the Reverend Francis Bernard, Rector of Brightwell, gave birth to a son, also named Francis. Both parents died by the time the child was seven years old and he was brought up by an aunt. After Winchester and Oxford, he married an aristocratic wife and settled down, comfortably enough at first, to practice law in the city of Lincoln.

By middle age, and with a family of eight children, Francis Bernard was forced to acknowledge that he would never earn enough as a provincial lawyer to live in a manner that matched his social aspirations. Calling on his wife's cousin, who happened to be Lord Barrington of the Colonial Office, he secured a position in the New World as Governor of the Province of New Jersey.

And so it was that in January of 1758 Francis and Amelia Bernard, with four of their children, set sail for North America.

At first, all went well. Governor Bernard seems to have been reasonably popular – the town of Bernardsville, New Jersey, is named after him. Eighteen months later, his connection with

Lord Barrington brought him further advancement, this time to the Governorship of Massachusetts.

In Boston, things again began well. After four years as Governor the future must have seemed even brighter when, on a cold February morning in 1763, he stepped out on to the balcony of the Boston Town House to announce the end of the French and Indian Wars (known to European history as the Seven Years War). To cheers, he informed the crowd that the fighting was over and that France had ceded to Britain all the lands east of the Mississippi.

As for the job of governing Massachusetts itself, Bernard seems to have anticipated no great difficulties. 'The People in general,' he wrote in a report to his patron, Lord Barrington, 'are as well inclined to his Majesty's Government, and as well satisfied with their subordination to Great Britain, as any Colony in America.'

Twelve years later, Francis Bernard had been recalled in disgrace and the American colonies, led by Massachusetts, were in open revolt against the Crown.

౸౸

The story of the American Revolution has been told a thousand times and its immediate causes are well known. The French and Indian Wars had been costly, and Parliament in London had decided to impose taxes on its North American colonies to help pay for their continued defence and administration. The protests that followed in Massachusetts soon found outstanding leaders in men like the brilliant Boston lawyer James Otis, who preached: 'Taxation without representation is tyranny.'

It was in his handling of these protests that the vicar's son from Brightwell-cum-Sotwell found himself out of his diplomatic depth. His high-handedness, his fits of pique at any challenge to his authority, his readiness to classify every protest as sedition, and his propensity to make personal enemies of men like James Otis, allowed the dispute to degenerate into bitter accusations of treachery and betrayal on both sides. The Governor interpreted the protests against the hated Stamp Tax as 'a conspiracy of designing men ... to tumble the government and bring it to the level of the very people'. James Otis, equally intemperate, whipped up the colonists with warnings that 'jealousies and designs were fermenting' in the minds of 'weak and wicked officials'.

To make things worse, there were constant rumours about the Governor's dubious land deals and cosy relationships with corrupt customs officers. According to John Adams, later to become second President of the United States, Governor Bernard was 'avaricious to a most infamous degree; needy at the same time, having a numerous family to provide for.'[5]

When, in the Spring of 1769, secret correspondence between the Governor and the Colonial Office in London reached the *Boston Gazette* it caused a sensation. Bernard was revealed as having grossly exaggerated the unrest in order to provoke Parliament into despatching British regulars to put down 'rebellion'. Worse, he was seen to be plotting reforms that would have emasculated the Massachusetts Assembly and left the colonists with little say in their own affairs. Judging this intolerable, the Massachusetts Assembly took the unprecedented step of calling for Bernard's impeachment so that 'he might be forever removed from the Government of the Province'.

Afraid for his family's safety, the Governor withdrew to a castle on a small island in Boston Harbour. So out of control had the situation become that he thought it might 'bring on a conflict which may prove the most detrimental and ruinous event which could happen to this people'.

The American Revolution proved more successful than that, but not before much blood had been shed and communities torn apart as the British government attempted to crush the rebellion and the colonists faced a stark choice between 'patriots' and 'loyalists', many of the latter eventually fleeing to Canada.

In an attempt to defuse the situation, Bernard was recalled to London to face the formal charges levelled by the Massachusetts Assembly. On the day of his departure, spontaneous celebrations broke out in Boston, culminating in the decorating of the Liberty Tree and the ringing of the town's bells. A message scored on a windowpane read: 'August 2d 1769. The infamas Govener left our town.' An unknown pamphleteer offered this additional epitaph:

> Oh Bernard, Great thy Villainy has been!
> Schem'd to destroy our Liberty and Peace:
> The Publick Eye attentively has seen
> Thy base Endeavours, and watch'd our Ease.

The Governor was gone, but the damage was done. The unrest and rioting in the streets continued sporadically until, on March 5th, 1770, the troops Bernard had been instrumental in persuading Parliament to send opened fire on the crowd, killing five civilians, in what became known as the Boston Massacre. Over the following five years, under the scarcely more popular Governorship of Thomas Hutchinson, relations between Crown and colony continued to deteriorate. One by one, and reluctantly in most cases, the colonists' leaders concluded that the only way forward was independence from Britain. As is well known, the decisive moment came on April 19th, 1775, when a party of British Redcoats was sent out from Boston to look for hidden weapons. Soon after dawn, they encountered local militias near the village of Lexington. The redcoats opened fire, killing eight of the colonists. Later that same morning, just outside the village of Concord, another skirmish saw two more colonists dead. This time, the order was given to return fire, an act of treason. Two British soldiers were killed. And it was this incident that was to be immortalised in Ralph Waldo Emerson's 'Concord Hymn', sung at the opening of the monument to the events of that day:

> *By the rude bridge that arched the flood,*
> *The flag to April's breeze unfurled,*
> *Here once embattled farmers stood*
> *And fired the shot heard round the world.*

Meanwhile back in London, the charges brought against Bernard were dismissed as groundless and, far from being disgraced, he became adviser on colonial affairs to the Prime Minister, Lord North. Always pressing for a harder line to be taken, he continued to be a hated figure on the other side of the Atlantic. At the height of the American Revolution, when the colonists drew up a register of 'notorious conspirators against the government', heading the list was the name of Sir Francis Bernard.

'The infamas Govener' – Sir Francis Bernard, Governor of the Massachusetts Bay Colony, and 'implacable arch-enemy of the American struggle for self-government'.
(*engraving after a portrait by John Singleton Copley*)

By all accounts, Bernard was an intelligent, well-educated man and a devoted husband and father. He was also a patron of the arts, and an amateur architect – designing Harvard Hall after the original burnt down in 1764. It could also be said, in his defence, that he was caught between the rock of Parliament's demands for taxes and the hard place of the colonists' reluctance to pay them. But history as often turns on personalities as on politics, and there is little doubt in the minds of historians of the period that Bernard's personality and prejudices helped to transform the colonists' protests into the American Revolution.

Perhaps, also, the animosities he aroused arose from a clash of old and new worlds. Sir Francis Bernard was thought by the colonists to be an English snob, infatuated by titles and aristocratic lineage – a man who believed there could be no better future for places like Massachusetts than to imitate the mother country in all things. An early historian of the United States, George Bancroft, commented that Bernard desired nothing less than 'the Anglicisation of colonial life.' A more recent biographer, Jordan Fiore, has accused the Governor of being unwilling to 'modify his devotion to English manners, customs, and political ideals'.

Such attitudes were bound to go down badly in Massachusetts. 'New England' was a place where a fresh start had been made, a place of sturdy, self-reliant individuals and communities, a place where caps were not doffed, knees not bent, and old servilities not willingly observed. It may also be the case that the same sense of English superiority blinded Bernard to the fact that men like James Otis and Sam and John Adams, with their plain names and plain manners, were intellectually more than a match for anything that Winchester and Oxford could produce.

Something of the spirit of this underlying conflict, and an insight into the intemperance that characterised both sides, can be glimpsed in the scorching oratory of Otis who took delight in savaging 'titles' and those he saw as 'superior flunkeys' like Sir Francis. In a speech described by the Governor as the most 'insolent ... treasonable declamation that perhaps was ever delivered,' Otis attacked the whole of the British Parliament in these words:

> Pray what are those Men? – They have Titles 'tis true, They are rais'd above those whom they are pleas'd to stile the Vulgar – they have Badges to distinguish themselves – the unthinking Multitudes are taught to reverence them as little Deities – for what? Not their Virtues sure. This cannot be the case – it is notoriously known there are no set of People under the Canopy of Heaven more venal, more corrupt and debauch'd in their Principles. Is it then for their Superiour learning? No, by no means. 'Tis true they are sent to the Universities of Oxford and Cambridge – and pray what do the Learn there? Why, nothing at all but Whoring, Smoaking and Drinking – a Pious setting out truly. Seven or Eight Years spent to a fine Purpose indeed ... what are those mighty Men that affect to give Laws to the Colonies? A parcel of Button-makers, Pan-makers, House Jockeys, Gamesters, Pensioners, Pimps and Whore Masters.[6]

Modern historians have been little kinder than the colonists in their assessment of the unfortunate Governor. The leading British expert, Colin Nicolson of Stirling University, concludes that 'To those Americans who risked their lives and property in civil war and rebellion against British rule ... Sir Francis Bernard was the apotheosis of British colonialism and an implacable arch-enemy of the American struggle for self-government.'

American historians have generally agreed with this assessment. The American website devoted to biographies of the leading characters of the Revolution comments: 'It is tempting to wonder how history might have changed if a more skilful governor had been in power during those crucial years.'[7]

Several images of the 'infamas govener' have survived. Two portraits were painted by the distinguished Boston-born artist John Singleton Copley. One was donated by the Governor to Harvard College Library, only to be mutilated by students protesting the arrival of British troops in Boston. The other was donated to Bernard's alma mater, Christ Church, Oxford, on the occasion of his receiving an honorary degree in 1772. An engraved copy of this portrait, showing a rather chubby, periwigged, nervous-looking Sir Francis is preserved among the personal papers of President John F. Kennedy.

Bernard died at Nether Winchenden in Buckinghamshire on June 16th, 1779, three years after the Second Continental Congress voted to approve the American Declaration of Independence. He is buried in St Mary's churchyard, Aylesbury.

The vicar's son from Brightwell-cum-Sotwell travelled far to play his part in history. But he did not forget his native Berkshire.[8] For it was Francis Bernard who gave the name of 'the Berkshires' to the western part of Massachusetts, now one of the loveliest and most fashionable parts of New England. No doubt the 'infamas govener' would have despaired to know that, even three hundred years later, the locals still have not learned how to pronounce it.

This essay is much indebted to Colin Nicolson's study the 'Infamas Govener': Francis Bernard and the Origins of the American Revolution (*Northeastern University Press: Boston, 2001*).

7

No Glimmer of God's Hand

Many artists have painted the Wittenham Clumps. But Paul Nash, one of the most important British painters of the twentieth century, was obsessed by them. Between his first visit as a boy and his death in 1946, he painted the Clumps twenty-six times. 'Ever since I remember them,' he wrote in his autobiography, 'the Clumps have meant something to me … They were the pyramids of my small world.'

It was when staying with an uncle in Sinodun House, just outside Wallingford, that Nash first walked here on Round and Fort Hills. From the first, he found them 'full of strange enchantments … a beautiful, legendary country haunted by old gods long forgotten'. Ever drawn to pre-historic sites – burial mounds, Iron Age forts, standing stone circles – he said of the Clumps, 'I felt their importance long before I knew their history.'

Much as I would like to sing the praises of Nash's paintings of the Clumps, I have to confess to being in an unmoved minority. Unfortunately for Nash, a similarly unenthusiastic view was taken by that doyen of art teachers Henry Tonks. Nash would later say of Tonks, 'With hooded stare and sardonic mouth, he hung in the air above me, like a tall question mark, moreover … of a derisive, rather than an inquisitive order. In cold discouraging tones he welcomed me to the Slade. It was evident he considered that neither the Slade, nor I, was likely to derive much benefit.'

Asked to leave after a year, Nash studied lithography and printmaking, dabbled in writing plays and poetry, and hesitated about what to do next. In August 1912, he wrote to a friend, 'I am going to Wallingford in Berkshire[9] and there hope to find

The first of Paul Nash's many portrayals of the Wittenham Clumps – *The Wood on the Hill,* 1912, Ashmolean Museum, Oxford

some fine things, those wonderful Downs and wild woods down by the river. I have haunted them often and now I am going to try and interpret some of their secrets.' The result was the sketch called *The Wood on the Hill, 1912* and the chalk and watercolour painting which, though titled *Wittenham Clumps,* is a view of nearby Brightwell Barrow.[10] And it was in making these two studies, here on the slopes of the Clumps, that Nash found what was to be his lifelong vocation. 'As I began to draw,' he wrote, 'I warmed to my task. For the first time, perhaps, I was tasting fully the savour of my own pursuit. The life of a landscape painter.' Nash may not have been Cezanne, but the Clumps were his Mont Sainte-Victoire.

At the outbreak of World War I, Nash volunteered, somewhat reluctantly, and was assigned to the Artists' Rifles whose duties included guarding the Tower of London. But in February 1917, after officer training, he was sent to the Front.

It was a strange time to arrive in Flanders. The fighting was at a lull. Spring was beginning to restore the landscape. And apart from the odd shell screaming overhead, all was quiet on the Western Front. Nash's first reaction seems to have been one of exhilaration: 'The morning filled with sunshine made everything look full of colour and alive,' he wrote to his new wife, Margaret. 'The larks were singing and a fresh wind made walking very refreshing. Never have I seen such curious beauty.'

Even after being deployed to the trenches, he continued to write in the same optimistic tone: 'I feel very happy these days, in fact, I believe I am happier in the trenches than anywhere out here. It sounds absurd but life has a greater meaning here and a new zest, and beauty is more poignant.' It seems a curious response to war, but is not unlike the feeling expressed by Rupert Brooke in the famous lines of his 1914 poem 'Peace':

Now, God be thanked Who has matched us with His hour,
And caught our youth, and wakened us from sleeping,
With hand made sure, clear eye, and sharpened power,
To turn, as swimmers into cleanness leaping

For Nash, it was perhaps more the visual stimulus rather than patriotic pride that stirred his sensibility: 'Oh these wonderful trenches at night, at dawn, at sundown,' he wrote of his early excursions to the front lines.

Of course, it was not to last. But just before the action began again, Nash fell into a trench, broke a rib, and was invalided home covered more in mud than glory. Less than a week later, his unit of the Hampshire Regiment was ordered to take the infamous Hill Sixty. Fewer than half survived.

After petitioning the War Propaganda Bureau for a posting as an official war artist, Nash returned to the Front towards the end of 1917, accompanied by a batman and a chauffeur. But the vision that greeted him now was changed, changed utterly, from the Flanders he had left. Three months of continuous shelling during the Third Battle of Ypres had destroyed the system of canals, ditches and dikes, and the weeks of rain had created a sea of mud and misery. 'Imagine a wide landscape,' he now wrote, 'flat and scantily wooded and what trees remain blasted and torn, naked and scarred and riddled, the ground for miles around furrowed into trenches, pitted with yawning holes in which water lies still and cold or heaped in mounds of earth, tangles of rusty wire, tin plates, stakes, sandbags and all the refuse of war.'

It was now that Nash experienced that same transformation of feeling, that same scarce-believing, all-encompassing horror and anger that had earlier overtaken the poetry of Siegfried Sassoon, Wilfred Owen and Isaac Rosenberg. The youths who had marched off to war were no longer like Brooke's 'swimmers into cleanness leaping', but like Owen's 'old beggars under sacks, knock-kneed, coughing like hags', and instead of the spirit of England awakening 'ardent-eyed' and 'dying gladly for thee' came the brutal realities of the trenches and some of the most graphic descriptions of war ever written:

Therefore still their eyeballs shrink tormented
Back into their brains, because on their sense
Sunlight seems a blood-smear; night comes blood-black;
Dawn breaks open like a wound that bleeds afresh.

From 'Mental Cases', Wilfred Owen

From this and many other verses of 1916 and 1917 came an outpouring of disillusionment, disgust and despair – of a scorn for the armchair warriors at home and a heart-piercing lament for the waste and the pity of it all. My subject, said Owen, is 'the pity of war, the pity war distilled.'

For Nash, too, the pity of war now took over his pen and his palette. In a letter sent home, along with sketches from the front lines, he speaks directly of this change in words that show his power as writer as well as painter:

> I have seen the most frightful nightmare of a country more conceived by Dante or Poe than by nature, unspeakable, utterly indescribable. In the fifteen drawings I have made I may give you some idea of its horror, but only being in it and of it can ever make you sensible of its dreadful nature and of what our men in France have to face. We all have a vague notion of the terrors of a battle, and can conjure up with the aid of some of the more inspired war correspondents and the pictures in the Daily Mirror some vision of battlefield; but no pen or drawing can convey this country–the normal setting of the battles taking place day and night, month after month. Evil and the incarnate fiend alone can be master of this war, and no glimmer of God's hand is seen anywhere. Sunset and sunrise are blasphemous, they are mockeries to man, only the black rain out of the bruised and swollen clouds all through the bitter black night is fit atmosphere in such a land. The rain drives on, the stinking mud becomes more evilly yellow, the shell holes fill up with green-white water, the roads and tracks are covered in inches of slime, the black dying trees ooze and sweat and the shells never cease. They alone plunge overhead, tearing away the rotting tree stumps, breaking the plank roads, striking down horses and mules, annihilating, maiming, maddening, they plunge into the grave, and cast up on it the poor dead. It is unspeakable, godless, hopeless.

Few artists have been called upon to make the switch from pastoral idyll to trench warfare, from the Wittenham Clumps to the Ypres Salient, but like the poets of the Great War, Nash faced up to the challenge and found his voice – horror and anger driving him on to make as many as a dozen sketches a day at the Front. In their depiction of uncompromising bleakness and despair, the studies for paintings like *Wire, After the Battle* and *The Menin Road* are the visual equivalent of the great war poems of the period. To take one example, the painting ironically titled *We Are Making a New World* shows a weak sunrise over the aftermath of battle; only now instead of the morning being 'filled with sunshine that made everything look full of colour and alive,' the sun is rising on a landscape of tortured, blackened, blasted trees that no sun could revive. Even more dramatic is *The Menin Road*, described by art critic Waldemar Januszczak as 'a vision of apocalyptic devastation'.

Worlds away from the Wittenham Clumps – *The Menin Road*, completed in 1919, depicts the blasted trees and water-filled shell craters that almost obscure the road from Ypres to Menin. Nash's large oil-on-canvas work, now in the Imperial War Museum, London, is one of the most famous images of the First World War.

≈≈

About the only thing that paintings like *The Menin Road*, *Sunrise* and *Inverness Copse* have in common with Nash's landscapes of the Oxfordshire countryside is that they are mostly paintings of trees.

The dominant features of the great works conceived in 1917 are the shattered and charred tree trunks reaching up hopelessly for lost life in a dead land. To some, it has seemed that the artist is more affected by the desecration of nature than by the sufferings of men, but in Nash's mind trees and human beings were almost interchangeable. In a letter written before the war, he explained that in painting trees, 'I have tried to paint as tho they were human beings ... because I sincerely love and worship trees and know they are people and wonderfully beautiful people – much more lovely than the majority of people one meets.' Eccentric, yes. But consistent to the end. Even his paintings of Wittenham's beeches – his 'swooning' trees – have an eerie human presence. And in his paintings from the Front, it is the trees that shriek of shattered lives.

In part, the explanation may be mundane: Nash had little talent for figure drawing. Yet it is impossible to look at his paintings from this time without feeling that he was projecting his despair and anger on to those trees; that the nature he depicts is crying out with anger and despair for humanity, and that the burnt and broken trees stand as harrowing symbols for Owen's 'the pity of war, the pity war distilled.'

All this, of course, was not what the War Propaganda Bureau wanted to see, any more than the poems of Sassoon and Owen were what they wanted to hear. But Nash no longer cared. Just as Sassoon's poems had moved away from patriotic platitudes to the cruel realities of the trenches, and just as Owen carried horrific photographs of the wounded to thrust in front of blowhards back home glorifying the war, so Nash produced drawings and paintings whose style and content defied what was expected of him. In another letter home, he defends the change:

I am no longer an artist interested and curious, I am a messenger who will bring back word from the men who are fighting to those who want the war to go on for ever. Feeble, inarticulate, will be my message, but it will have a bitter truth, and may it burn their lousy souls.

Nash therefore became one of the first to develop war art into an art of protest, pioneering a genre that reached its most famous expression in Picasso's *Guernica*.

There were pioneers, also, on the other side of the trenches. Only a year or two younger than Nash, the German artist Otto Dix fought in the Battle of the Somme and used that experience to paint the evils of war. And his message was just as unwelcome in Berlin. Paintings like *Trench Warfare* earned him disdain for being unpatriotic, so much so that his work was included in the Nazi's 1937 exhibition of 'Degenerate Art'. The work of another German, Käthe Kollwitz, is perhaps even more remarkable. Breaking into the almost exclusively male preserve of war art, Kollwitz's images of bereaved and grieving wives and mothers, and her tributes to the contributions and the sufferings of women in wartime, took the genre to new heights. Sculptures like *Pietà* and *Mother with Her Dead Son* and woodcuts like *The Widow* are some of the most powerful examples of war art ever created, made all the more poignant by the fact that Kollwitz's own son, Peter, was killed in World War I and that she lived to see her grandson, also called Peter, killed in World War II.

Nash, too, lived to see the world go to war again. In 1939, he was once more appointed as an official war artist. And once more his paintings failed to find favour with his paymasters. Partly this was because of the modernist style, but it was also because the Air Ministry wanted portraits of its heroic aircrews and Nash wanted to paint downed German aircraft in the English countryside. A year into the war, his contract was ended.

Swayed by the art historian Kenneth Clark, the Ministry continued to buy the occasional Nash painting, including *Totes Meer (Dead Sea)*. This, his most famous work from the period, was painted from a point overlooking the Metal and Produce Recovery Depot at Cowley, on the edge of Oxford, where wrecks of both German and British planes were brought for salvage. Nash shows this vast aircraft graveyard as rhythmic waves of wrecked wings, wheels and propellers appearing to lap up onto a beach under a pale moon. Choosing to include only the wrecks of Luftwaffe planes, he gave the painting the German title *Totes Meer* because he wanted it to be reproduced on postcards and air-dropped over Berlin. The suggestion was not taken up.

By 1942, Nash's asthma was becoming chronic. After a spell in hospital, he went to stay at the home of a friend on Boar's Hill, Oxford. There, from his south-facing window, he had a view over Bagley Woods towards the Wittenham Clumps. Using binoculars to close the eight-mile distance, he began a final series of paintings of the twin hills. The most famous of these, *Landscape of the Vernal Equinox*, shows sun and moon simultaneously rising over a surrealist version of the Clumps topped by their beech trees. It was bought by Queen Elizabeth the Queen Mother and now hangs in the National Gallery of Scotland.

And so it was that Nash's life as a landscape painter ended as it began, with paintings that attempted to portray the Wittenham Clumps and 'what they meant to me'.

Nash and the Clumps

More than seventy years after his death, the memory of Nash's affinity with the Wittenham Clumps is kept alive by a dedicated website curated by Anna Dillon and Christopher Baines: www.nashclumps.org. The website features Nash's paintings of the Clumps alongside photographs showing the changes that have overtaken the landscape in the century or so since he first set up his easel here. A fine landscape artist in her own right, Anna Dillon has also painted the Clumps many times, using thin layers of oil paint to build the contours into harmonies of colour and light. In 2013, she began a series of paintings showing what has become of the World War I battlefields that Nash believed would never recover.

A new book (2020) by Christopher Baines – *Pyramids in England* – also explores Paul Nash's long association with the Wittenham Clumps.

Paul Nash's letters to his wife from the Western Front are included in Outline, Nash's unfinished autobiography. A new edition, *Paul Nash: Outline, an Autobiography*, edited by David Boyd Haycock, was published to coincide with Tate Modern's major Paul Nash retrospective in 2016 (Lund Humphries Ltd, 2016).

II

LIFE MAY BE CHEERED

Illustration: Sarah Woolfenden

*'Among many other valuable lessons, Mr Clutterbuck
has taught us how life may be cheered and brightened
by cultivating habits of observation and reflection on
what we see around us in our everyday life.'*

Sir John Hoskyns, *The Wallingford Times*, May 20th, 1885,
(Letter in response to the obituary of the Rev. J. C. Clutterbuck,
vicar of Long Wittenham, 1830–1885).

8

TUBB, OR NOT TUBB

The smooth trunks of beech trees have always invited the carving of initials and dates, loves and hates. Even Classical Rome had 'beech-scribblers' whose sappy favourite was: '*Crescent illae, crescit amores.*' ('As these letters grow so will our love.') So it is not surprising that most of the older beeches on the Wittenham Clumps bear the marks of this temptation. On Fort Hill, there is even a graffito carved in Latin, though most of us could probably manage '*Te Amo*'.

Joseph Tubb went further. Much further. On a summer evening in the year 1844, the middle-aged bachelor from Warborough left home carrying a knife and a wooden ladder. Crossing the Thames at Day's Lock and passing through Church Meadow, he climbed Fort Hill and propped the ladder against the trunk of a hundred-year-old beech tree. There he took out a sheet of paper on which was written a poem – and began transcribing it into the bark.

On many a fine evening over the next two summers, Tubb could be seen on his ladder at the south-east corner of the hill, gradually working his way down the trunk of the long-suffering beech. By the time he was finished, the twenty lines of heroic couplets covered half the girth of the tree to a height of about two metres.

In much the same way that time can upgrade outlaws to saints, Joseph Tubb's act of vandalism eventually came to be revered as the 'Poem Tree'. Stopping to decipher a few lines, walkers on the Clumps would often look out from this spot and, in the words of the poem itself:

Point out each object and instructive tell
The various changes that the land befell.

Tubb had always wanted to be a woodcarver. But his father had insisted on his entering the family business of making malt for local brewers. For this reason, some have seen the carving of the poem as a symbol of irrepressible creativity overcoming the pressures of conformity. Others have concluded that Tubb Snr was probably right to advise his son not to give up the day job.

For the next century and a half, the 'Poem Tree' flourished on the Clumps, a well-known landmark, picnic spot, and lovers' rendezvous, though by 1870 the words had already become difficult to read. At around that time, a Mr Mowat of Pembroke College, Oxford, transcribed the poem. But it was not until another twenty years had passed that it was first published – in *The Berkshire Archaeological Journal* – under the title 'Lines cut on a beech tree on Sinodun Hill' (an old name for the Clumps).

The poem tree – A hundred and fifty years after they were carved, the words of Joseph Tubb's poem had become almost indecipherable.
(photograph: Matt Girling, Creative Commons Share Alike 3.0).

By the last decade of the twentieth century, the tree was visibly ailing. Old age was the problem, probably not helped by so many deep cuts into the inner layer of bark – known as the phloem – that carries the nutrients and sugars from roots to branches. Some arborists maintain that carving on tree trunks does little harm. But whether or not the phloem was damaged by the poem and the tree the worse for verse, the turn of the twenty-first century saw the great beech rotting where it stood, the trunk decaying from within, the ageing bark distorting the letters and rendering Joseph Tubb's poem as difficult to decipher as a dead sea scroll.

It was on a stormy night in the summer of 2012 that the tree finally came crashing down, or at least as far down as a precarious resting place against a sturdy hawthorn. Soon afterwards, a crane was brought up to winch its remains gently to the ground. But just as the chains began to cradle its weight, the trunk collapsed, scattering decayed heartwood and forlorn fragments of Tubb's verses all around.

The poem itself, however, survived, thanks to the various transcriptions and the tracing made by Henry Osmaston.

❧

Osmaston might be said to have had a varied career: he was born in the Himalayas, educated at Eton, and was at various times forester, mountaineer, elephant rider, ornithologist, electrician, dairy farmer, university lecturer, and organiser of the first Ugandan skiing championships. One day in 1965, he found time for a stroll on the Wittenham Clumps where he came across Tubb's poem. Seeing that it would not be long before the lines became indecipherable, he hit upon the idea of tracing the trunk of the tree.

It was the sort of notion that many of us might have had, but never quite got around to doing anything about. Osmaston was different. Even colleagues seemed to think his tirelessness exhausting. Returning to the Clumps with a large polythene sheet, he persuaded his two children to hold the sheet around the tree while he traced the poem with a marker pen. And it is Osmaston's tracing of the text, now cast in bronze and set into a large boulder from the gravel pits at Sutton Courtenay, that can be seen today on the spot where the 'Poem Tree' once stood. There are minor variations between different transcriptions of the poem. This is Henry Osmaston's version:

> As up the hill with labr'ing steps we tread
> Where the twin Clumps their sheltering branches spread
> The summit gain'd at ease reclining lay
> And all around the wide spread scene survey
> Point out each object and instructive tell
> The various changes that the land befell
> Where the low bank the country wide surrounds
> That ancient earthwork form'd old Mercia's bounds
> In misty distance see the barrow heave
> There lies forgotten lonely Cwichelm's grave.
>
> Around this hill the ruthless Danes intrenched
> And these fair plains with gory slaughter drench'd
> While at our feet where stands that stately tower
> In days gone by up rose the Roman power
> And yonder, there where Thames smooth waters glide
> In later days appeared monastic pride.
> Within that field where lies the grazing herd
> Huge walls were found, some coffins disinter'd
> Such is the course of time, the wreck which fate
> And awful doom award the earthly great.

❧❧

Tubb's verses are not the only poem to be inspired by the Clumps. The long, not to say interminable, eighteenth-century love poem 'Henry and Emma' is said to have been written by Matthew Prior as he sat under one of the Wittenham oak trees. The poem was widely read in its time and is generally credited with launching the popularity of the name Emma. It is now most often encountered in the mention made of it in Jane Austen's novel *Persuasion*: 'emulating the feelings of an Emma to her Henry'.

The need to write such poetry seems to arise from sensations for which everyday language is insufficient. Something special is called for. And poetry, with its patterns of metre and rhyme, and more discriminating use of words, seems to answer the call. In the case of Joseph Tubb, looking out from the Clumps over hundreds of square miles of Oxfordshire and Berkshire, his response had to do with his sense of a landscape existing in time as well as in space. As his eyes travel across the plain to the Chilterns and the Downs, his thoughts also reach back, wondering at all that has come to pass in these acres, from the Iron Age to the Roman occupation, from the coming of Christianity to the rise of the Mediaeval monasteries.

Surprisingly, given the effort involved, the poem is unsigned and there is no contemporary evidence that Tubb was its author. Not until the 1881 edition of *The History of Wallingford in the County of Berks* – published two years after Tubb's death and thirty-six years after the poem's carving – is the existence of a 'Poem Tree' on the Wittenham Clumps first recorded. But even this mention, including a complete transcript of the poem, does not say who wrote the lines. Discussing the mystery in the pages of *Jackson's Oxford Journal* in 1890, some said the author was a London coachbuilder who had been visiting a friend in Dorchester. Others maintained it was a local shepherd who had carved the lines during lonely days on the hill. Another ten years were to pass before a notice appeared in the *Berkshire*

Archaeological Journal attributing the poem to Joseph Tubb.
The key entry reads:

> Mr Henry J. Hewett writes to say that the lines were
> composed and carved by the late Mr Joseph Tubb, of
> Warborough Green. He did the work in his leisure time on
> occasional summer evenings in 1844 and 1845. There are
> discrepancies between the MS, now in possession of Mr Ben
> Tubb, of Brightwell,[11] Bucks, and the lines on the tree, which
> are due to the inscriber occasionally leaving the MS behind
> him, and cutting out a line from memory.[12]

Despite the fact that the writer obviously knew the family
(Tubb did indeed have a younger brother called Benjamin) and
that the letter specifically states that the poem was 'carved and
composed' by Joseph Tubb, the attribution of the poem has
occasionally been challenged.

One suggestion is that the lines might have been carved by
Tubb but written by someone else. It has also been speculated that
it was derived from another work in circulation at the time –
'Wittenham-Hill, a Poem' penned in 1771 by Thomas Pentycross,
vicar of St Mary-le-More, Wallingford, whose portly image is
preserved in an engraving in the archives of the National Portrait
Gallery. But after tracking down a copy of this deservedly obscure
poem I can find nothing in its twelve pages of versifying to suggest
that it inspired Joseph Tubb or anybody else.

The main argument against Tubb's authorship seems to be
that a man whose business was germinating, drying and
malting grain was unlikely to know about Roman, Saxon and
Mediaeval history. But this is surely unconvincing. Then, as
now, there were people of all occupations who were knowledgeable about the history of their local areas. It is also known that
Tubb was sufficiently interested in the past to have become
involved in protests against the Enclosure Acts, which deprived

local villagers of their historic rights to the use of common land. At one point, he was briefly held in Oxford jail for ripping up fences by which such acts were enforced.

So, objection overruled. As far as we can know, Joseph Tubb Esq., political protester and malt maker of Warborough Green, Oxfordshire, was the author and carver of the poem. And anyone determined enough to deface a tree with over seven hundred and fifty separate letters cut into the bark, yet self-effacing enough not to add two more to prove his authorship, surely deserves his modest fame.

A note on the places referred to in Joseph Tubb's poem

The 'ancient earthwork that form'd old Mercia's bounds' is generally taken to refer to Grim's Ditch, which formed part of the boundary between the two Anglo-Saxon kingdoms of Wessex and Mercia. But Grim's Ditch – a Bronze Age earthwork best seen between Mongewell and Nuffield on the Ridgeway Path – is only just visible from the 'Poem Tree', even on a good day. So, depending on just how keen a historian Tubb was, he might have believed that 'old Mercia's bounds' were marked by the much nearer Dyke Hills, an Iron Age earthwork, now much damaged, situated between the Clumps and Dorchester Abbey.

'Lonely Cwichelm's grave' is more obscure. What little is known about Cwichelm comes from The Anglo-Saxon Chronicle, which names him as one of the earliest Kings of Wessex. His main claim to fame was that, like King Cynegils (presumed to be his father), he was baptised in the river Thames by Bishop Birinus who had been sent by the Pope to convert the West Saxons. Birinus clearly reasoned that if Cynegils and his successor, Cwichelm, could be brought to Christ then the whole of the royal court, retainers, dependents, serfs, and so on, were also likely to see the light. The baptism of Cynegils and Cwichelm (in the same year, 636) was therefore a significant moment in the Christianisation of England. But again, the earthwork 'barrow' known as Scutchmer Knob, where it is assumed that Cwichelm is buried, is ten miles away on the Downs and I have struggled to locate it using binoculars. Could Tubb have mistaken it for Brightwell Barrow, staring him at a distance of only half a mile as he looked up from his carving? The poem does describe Cwichelm's grave as being 'In misty distance' – so, once again, Tubb gets the benefit of the doubt.

'Around this hill the ruthless Danes intrenched' refers to the Viking invasion of Wessex in 869. On that occasion, the Danes were paid off by Alfred the Great, only to return five years later. This time Alfred paid them in steel rather than gold, eventually defeating the Danish army at the Battle of Edington. This, too, was a crucial moment, paving the way for the unification of England under Alfred's grandson.

The 'stately tower' is that of Dorchester Abbey, easily visible then as now from the Clumps. 'In days gone by up rose the Roman power' refers to the Roman fortification of Dorchester in the second century. 'Monastic pride' also refers to the Abbey, founded by Augustinian monks in 1140 (the tower was rebuilt in 1602).

9

Love at First Click

As I sit on a bench at the top of Round Hill, I can see below me a young couple unlatching the gate opposite Little Wittenham church. Behind them, in the lane, the lights of their car blink once in the gathering dusk as they stroll, hand in hand, towards me across Church Meadow.

The village they are leaving behind, marked by a hundred-foot poplar tree, could easily be the setting for any one of Jane Austen's novels, Emma's Highbury perhaps, or Lizzie Bennet's Longbourn. Indeed a great many of the villages around the Clumps have the basic scenery for an Austen drama: a manor, or 'great house', a parish church and a rectory, some humbler half-timbered cottages, perhaps a row of alms houses, and one or two outlying farms that could be home to *Emma*'s Robert Martin.

Much has changed, of course: the barouche-landau has given way to the Range Rover; the muddy cart track to today's tarmac; Mr and Mrs Elton to the Revd Sue Booys; the poorhouse, workhouse and alms-house to the pension and the welfare state; scavenging ravens and kites for green bins and weekly refuse collection; fleas, vermin and foul 'airs' to new standards of hygiene and cleanliness; Mr Collins' precious tithes for the graduated income tax. Not least, Mr Woodhouse's trusted apothecary, Perry, has been replaced by a practice team of GPs backed up by Oxford's John Radcliffe Hospital, whose distant buildings can just be seen from up here on the Hill.

Some of the changes are so taken for granted that we no longer feel their revolutionary edge. The young couple now crossing Church Meadow, for example, can reasonably expect to live into their nineties; the young couples of Jane Austen's novels – Elizabeth Bennet and Fitzwilliam Darcy, say, or Elinor Dashwood and Edward Ferrars – faced a high probability of dying in their forties; Jane herself died at the age of forty-one. Any children born to the young couple below, supposing they continue to be as fond of each other as they currently appear, will have a better than ninety-nine per cent chance of surviving to adulthood. Any children born to Lizzie and Darcy would have faced a one-in-three chance of dying before the age of five.

If this young couple marry, then unlike Jane Austen's heroines the woman will not have to surrender her property and even her legal existence to her husband. And unlike the women of Mary Wollstonecraft's *A Vindication of the Rights of Woman*, written soon after the planting of the Wittenham Clumps, she will not have to lament: 'How many women … waste life away, the prey of discontent, who might have practiced as physicians, regulated a farm, managed a shop, and stood erect, supported by their own industry, instead of hanging their heads?' By and large, she will have the same kind of education, and the same right to a job, income and pension as her partner. She will have a female doctor to go to. She will have a choice of safe, effective methods of birth control. And if she does not always get along as well with her partner as she appears to be doing at the moment, then she will have the right to divorce.

In the village they are leaving behind, where the first lights are now beginning to appear in windows, average incomes are fifteen to twenty times higher in real terms than in the Georgian era, an increase far greater than in all the preceding centuries. And that means infinitely better housing, furniture, lighting, water supply, sanitation, transport, opportunities for travel, education, leisure and entertainment, and a variety of foods that would have astonished the good citizens of Highbury or Longbourn.

But of all of the changes since Jane Austen wrote *Pride and Prejudice* just over two centuries ago, perhaps none is so profound as that represented by the young couple themselves as they begin to climb, still hand-in-hand, up the broad, grassy track towards where I sit here at the top of Round Hill. It is not merely that they are unchaperoned, or the impropriety of their dress, or the lack of all modesty in the young woman's deportment, or even the shameless display of affection as they turn and admire the view. No, the true significance of the scandalous scene before me resides in the fact that this young couple have almost certainly not been properly introduced.

The formal introduction was the principal means by which parents of Jane Austen's day sought to ensure that their sons and daughters did not form unsuitable attachments. Without an introduction – by a family member or mutual acquaintance in good standing – young people of the time could not converse or dance with each other, could not be alone together, could not go for a walk or write letters to each other, could not even use each other's Christian names.

The tension between these cold conventions of control and the spontaneous feelings of the young was the mainspring of Jane Austen's plots: girl meets boy, love dawns, social and material considerations throw obstacles in the way until prejudice and snobbery are eventually overcome by the forces of romantic attraction currently being flagrantly displayed here on the lower slopes of Round Hill.

This is the process that was put under the lens of Austen's irony, mocking the snobberies and pretensions of the society in which she lived and wrote. But for all the subtle scorn, Austen is not out to subvert the rituals of the class system. Board school orphan Harriet Smith may not aspire to Mr Knightley; she must stay within her own sphere and marry the respectable farmer Robert Martin. Even in the most famous of all love-overcomes-distinctions-of-rank stories, Elizabeth Bennet defends herself against Lady Catherine's accusation that she inhabits a different social sphere from Darcy – and that their attachment would 'pollute the shades of Pemberley' – by replying, 'In marrying your nephew, I should not consider myself as quitting that sphere. He is a gentleman; I am a gentleman's daughter; so far we are equal.'

No, the basic divisions of the Georgian class system are to remain intact: it is only within their bounds that discrepancies in wealth and rank may be overcome by the vaulting of the heart. And that, of course, was what all the rules and rituals were designed to uphold. The limited opportunities for meeting, the necessity of a formal introduction, the imperative of the chaperone, the close supervision of 'coming out' – all were put in place to preserve social and material status. Cumulatively, they preserved the class system itself.

The young couple below, who have now resumed their climb and are conducting themselves with a little more decorum, face no such obstacles. They were able to meet freely at school or college, office or factory, bar or restaurant, pub or party, or through a common interest or mutual friend. But it is also possible, perhaps even probable, that their introduction to each other did not happen in the real world at all.

Although the first internet dating services did not appear until 1995, online match-up sites like 'Match', 'Tinder' and 'Eharmony' are now running a close second to 'through friends' as the most common way for young men and women to meet each other. In the United States, things have gone further – with more than a third of all new marriages now beginning with online contact. In India, websites like Matrimony.com are taking over from the small ads in newspapers. In China, Tantan.com has twenty million users and claims to have 'created' ten million couples.

Having recently celebrated my golden wedding anniversary, I cannot claim extensive personal experience of internet dating services. But it is not hard to understand their popularity. If the young couple now climbing towards me had met in pub or office, for example, then they would have had at most a few dozen people from which to choose. Online, they have thousands. And not only is the choice far wider, but the process is arguably fairer, outdating the old distinction between the man's power of proposition and the woman's power of rejection.

Not least, match-up sites also make it possible to specify what kind of person you might be interested in meeting. You can specify, for example, a postgraduate education, or an interest in theatre. You can prioritise people who are tall or blonde or gay or Asian or Jewish, and even filter out those who would not consider converting to Judaism. You can filter for book lovers or outdoor types, cyclists or farmers, conservatives or vegans. A woman can screen out all men except those willing to father a child and disappear. There is even a match-up site called theUglyBugBall.com, which advertises itself as 'dating for the aesthetically average'.

Swipe right to subvert the social order?

All of this offers many advantages, not least for those whose preferences have until recently been a matter of secrecy or shame. Almost three-quarters of same-sex couples in the United States, for example, now meet their partners online. As an added benefit, online match-ups can also help to free people from their social and ethnic silos and bring together those who might otherwise have fewer opportunities for getting to know each other. And compared to the rituals and awkwardnesses of the past, it's all so simple. All that the users of the dating app Tinder have to do is to look at other users on their phones and swipe right for 'yes' and left for 'no'; any two people who swipe right on each other are then put in contact. Or at least it's simple to begin with.

Hard as it is to imagine Jane Austen sitting at her little table in the window at Chawton swiping through images of potential suitors, she would not have been entirely unfamiliar with the concept. In Georgian times it was not uncommon for men and women of all social classes to place ads offering marriage in newspapers (though it was considered a little indelicate and possibly indicative of desperation).

What would have surprised Jane more is the classlessness of today's means of arranging introductions. Even the small ads of her own time invariably led off with the socio-economic standing of the applicant: 'Middle-aged gentleman of respectable rank in life who enjoys an income of Two Hundred pounds a Year.' Today's match-up sites are unlikely to feature social rank, and as Jane right-swipes her way through Matchup.com she is no doubt concluding that the whole process is designed to subvert rather than shore up the social order.

She would have noticed, however, that match-up sites do tend to give prominence to educational status: 'Arts graduate working in publishing seeks...' or 'Bookish postgraduate GBM currently working in IT ...' Incidentally, acronyms like GBM (Gay Black Male) are strewn across internet dating sites and can be very confusing. I naively assumed, for example, that MBA meant Master of Business Administration, but am reliably informed that it means Married But Available. Clearly, a degree of caution is needed.

In short, it can be argued that the couple now labouring up the last and steepest part of the climb – and once again behaving in a manner which may best be described as 'informal' – represent not the sweeping away of class distinction based on birth but its replacement by a class system based on education. Give or take, in Jane's day you married someone of your own social class, whereas today you pair-off with someone of your own educational class. Graduates are more likely to marry other graduates; those with no qualifications are more likely to marry each other.

This trend, known to economists by the uncomfortable sounding name of 'assortative mating', was established before the advent of the internet. But match-up sites are making it much more efficient.

Does all this matter? Doesn't it just help young people avoid the plight of a Mr Bennet whose life is plagued because he married a woman of the same social class but of 'far inferior understanding'? (He all but confesses to this mistake when he advises Lizzie with the words 'Your lively talents would place you in the greatest danger in an unequal marriage ... My child, let me not have the grief of seeing you unable to respect your partner in life.')

But, yes, it matters. And it will probably come to matter even more.

The contrast between the class consciousness of the Georgian era and the supposed 'classless society' is perhaps not as great as we think. Two hundred years ago, your social status and economic prospects could be roughly predicted by knowing the circumstance of your birth; today, it is educational attainment that best predicts what your economic standing will be, what dinner parties you will be invited to, what kind of house and community you will live in, how you live, spend, speak, dress, eat, behave, and relate to other people.

✌✎

In many ways, the new class system of our own time is far more formidable than the version that provided Jane Austen and her generations of readers with so much amusement. That old class structure was swept away because it had no real foundations. It was an artificial edifice, built not on real differences between people but on the mere accident of being born into a particular family, one or more of whose ancestors had at some time in the past been lucky, brutal or brave. Being without foundations, it had to be propped up by pretensions and pomposities, by titles and ceremonies, by arcane rules and rituals, by arbitrary intricacies of etiquette and pitiful notions of 'blue blood', by the absurdities of accent and manner and pass-the-port-this-way-and-not-that and all the other prissy, precious markers of class distinction that provided such a rich seam for Jane Austen's sly, ironic eye.

By contrast, the system that has replaced it *is* based on something real. 'Blue blood' is a myth; that some people have higher levels of certain abilities is not a myth. And to make today's class system even more formidable, traits like intelligence and conscientiousness are, like all human traits, influenced by genetic inheritance. In other words, the new class system has a genuinely hereditary component which the old class system, for all its concern about 'good breeding', did not.

The upside is obvious. A modern complex society needs its most able people in its top positions, whether in business or politics or science or health care. No one is anxious to see nobly born incompetents with their hands on the levers of power. The downside is more controversial. The tendency to choose partners of approximately the same educational level leads inexorably to more households with two highly educated high-income earners, and correspondingly more households with two less well-educated low-income earners. There are many exceptions and many other causes of inequality in today's globalised economy, but 'assortative mating' is one reason for the widening gap between rich and poor.

Unfortunately, the impetus to inequality does not stop there. Two parents with higher educational levels and higher incomes are also likely to be able to provide their children with many other advantages. So the children of those in the upper echelons of the new class system are likely to be the beneficiaries of environmental as well as genetic advantage.

At the moment, this process of assortative mating is imprecise and fallible. But the algorithms of online match-up sites are rendering it ever more sophisticated. Before long, it will be possible to upload an individual's polygenic score to the internet, so allowing those who want to improve their chances of having highly intelligent children to base their choice of mate on something more precise and measurable. In the meantime, in the United States, they are making do with dating sites open only to graduates of ivy league universities.

This, in the end, is why the young couple now heading towards my bench may represent the most profound of all the changes since Jane Austen's time. If they are at all typical of young couples today, then they embody the age-old story of girl-meets-boy in its new role as a means of consolidating a meritocratic class system that is likely to prove far more resistant to change than the empty notions of rank and status so zealously but ineffectually defended by Lady Catherine de Bourgh or Sir Walter Elliot.

Coming back to earth, the light is fading fast now and the young couple in whom I have vested so much speculation have arrived at the path that circles the top of the Clumps. We exchange a polite 'good evening', as people always do when walking the Earth Trust lands, but my British reserve does not allow me to ask how they met and whether they are of similar educational level. This is, after all, Wittenham Clumps, not Beverley Hills.

10

POWER VIEWING

Sit with me a while on the Steve Freeman memorial bench at the top of Round Hill from where we have a fine view over five or six hundred square miles of Oxfordshire and Berkshire. And also a view of two great examples of human enterprise: one that has made possible the world of today, and one that could make possible the world of tomorrow.

For almost half a century, the view from this spot was dominated by the giant paraboloid cooling towers of Didcot A Power Station. Back in the 1960s, there were public protests against putting the towers up. Forty years later, there were public protests against pulling them down. Neither had the slightest effect. And so it was here, just after dawn on Sunday, July 27th, 2014, that a crowd of several hundred gathered to await the moment when explosive charges, packed into over eight thousand holes drilled into the bases of three of the six towers, were detonated by remote radio signal. Less than ten seconds later, thirty-six thousand tonnes of concrete and steel had been reduced to rubble and dust.

On another Sunday morning, five years later, a crowd again assembled on this spot to witness the destruction of the three remaining towers. Some had brought thermos flasks and portable barbecues, and the smell of frying bacon caught the early morning air as the moment neared. Again, there was the distant flicker of light, followed by the ominous, far-off crump of dynamite – then a moment when time itself seemed to hesitate before the three towers buckled slowly, agonisingly, descending to the earth in a cloud of dust that drifted gently off towards the south.

Our familiar landmark was gone.

There were a few cheers and some half-hearted applause on the Clumps that morning. But also an undeniable sense of something lost. The readers of *Country Life* may have voted Didcot Power Station third in the list of 'Britain's worst eyesores', but many of us had come to regard it almost with affection over the years. Visible for miles in all directions, it was the great cooling towers that first said 'home' whenever we returned from our travels. And to walkers on the Clumps, it was a source of fascination to see how the changing light and atmosphere made the towers seem sometimes so near and sometimes so far away. Local artists and photographers, too, had been captivated by the play of light on their sculptural forms, not forgetting the poet Kit Wright and his 'Ode to Didcot Power Station'.

With all six towers of Didcot A now gone, the familiar landscape seems strangely unfamiliar, like coming across an elderly relative who has forgotten to put in his teeth.

I suppose we should be grateful. It was the 1997 Kyoto Conference on Climate Change that brought the great towers down. The UK could not meet its Kyoto commitment to reducing CO_2 emissions if it carried on generating so much of its electricity by burning coal. And Didcot A did burn coal: around fifteen thousand tonnes of it every day, hauled in by dusty trains from the coalfields of South Wales. On a rough calculation, this one power plant was thrusting five million tonnes of CO_2 into the skies of Oxfordshire each year.

Yes, Didcot A had to go. But here on Round Hill is also a good spot from which to remember for a moment all that coal has given us. Dirty and dangerous it has always been, but it was coal that led Britain and the world into the industrial age, making possible the smelting of iron and the powering of machinery, the steamships and railways, and the lighting and heating of factories, offices, shops and homes. For nearly half a century, Didcot A played its part in this great enterprise and Jim Haggan, its last station manager, was right to ask us to take a moment to salute 'this marvellous old workhorse.'

Next to the spot where the vanished towers stood is Didcot B, whose turbines continue to produce electricity but whose buildings offer only unshapely chimneys by way of a landmark. Being gas-fired, Didcot B is cleaner. But gas still puts CO_2 into the atmosphere. Some have even argued that, when leakage of methane from drilling and pipelines is taken into account, natural gas is just as climate-threatening as coal.

So for a future free of fossil fuel, we will have to look beyond Didcot B. And if we do look beyond, either with binoculars or exceptionally good eyesight, it is just possible to make out, on the horizon twenty miles away, five slowly turning wind turbines.

Power up the laptop. Open Google Earth. Plot a line from Wittenham Clumps through Didcot B. Project the line. Locate the turbines, easily found by their shadows. Look for the nearest village. Enter 'Denchfield' and 'wind turbines' into Google. Start reading about the Westmill Combined Solar and Wind Farm.

The gate is open and the field itself unremarkable, except for the five turbines spaced out on the grass of a long-abandoned airstrip. I gaze up in some awe at the slim white blades sweeping serenely, noiselessly above in only a slight breeze. There are no prohibition notices, no bars or warnings across the metal stair-cases by which I ascend five metres or so up the outsides of the turbine shafts. And from this point, just for confirmation, my binoculars search the horizon due east and come to rest on the faint outline of the Wittenham Clumps.

It is, I suppose, a sign of our conditioning to an industri-alised world that it takes a while to sink in that these tirelessly turning aerofoils, so constant and purposeful, are powered not by any underground motor but by the gentle movement of the same air that I feel on my face. Following the track around, I pass more turbines, each one named by local primary school children – 'Gusty Gizmo', 'Huff 'n Puff' – to arrive at a scrubby field where thirty acres of polycrystalline photovoltaic panels are raised at an angle, like an audience for the sun. On leaving, a modest notice by the gate announces that the site is owned by two thousand members of the community and that the five wind turbines and twenty-one thousand, six hundred solar panels provide enough electricity to meet the needs of four thousand homes.

✑

Impressive as Westmill Farm is, there are those who argue that wind and solar power cannot meet the world's massive and ever-growing needs for domestic and industrial energy. Billions of the world's citizens are not content to wash their clothes in rivers, cook their meals on three-stone fires, work their lands with hoes, light their homes with kerosene, travel to market on foot, or move their goods on carts. Billions more have their sights set on the living standards of America or Europe whose lifestyles they can tune into at the touch of an icon. If, as seems likely, we will need mega power stations to meet these demands, then we can look to the potential of nuclear fusion. And from this same bench at the top of Round Hill, it requires scarcely a turn of the head.

At first sight, the anonymous white buildings just below Wittenham Clumps could be an office block or a hospital. But inside the complex, scientists and engineers are testing and refining one of the world's most advanced scientific experiments. Not three miles from where I now sit on Round Hill is a chamber that can heat plasma to a temperature of one hundred and fifty million degrees Celsius – ten times hotter than the centre of the sun.

Once in a while, the Culham Centre for Fusion Energy – the research arm of the UK Atomic Energy Authority – hosts an open evening at which small groups of a dozen visitors are guided around by members of staff. Towards the end, the tour brings you face to face with the largest set of double doors you are ever likely to see – each perhaps twenty metres high and made of metre-thick concrete. Inside, surrounded by gantries, is what looks like a clumsy lunar landing module. This is the Joint European Torus which, when powered up, can generate magnetic fields powerful enough to control and manipulate the unthinkable temperatures and energy released when super-heated atoms of deuterium and tritium are fused. In matter-of-fact tones, our guide tells us that what happens inside the torus is the same process that powers the sun and the stars. But of course it is difficult for us visitors to truly comprehend – how can one kilogram of deuterium and tritium produce as much energy as ten thousand tonnes of coal?

Culham is not a power station. As at 2020, it is the world's largest fusion experiment, producing more actual energy from nuclear fusion than has ever been achieved before. But at this stage, it is still trying to establish the feasibility of the process as a source of electricity for the future. The next step is being taken near the small village of Saint-Paul-lès-Durance in the South of France where a torus ten times bigger than Culham's is being built by a consortium of thirty-five nations. This enterprise, known as the International Tokamak Experimental Reactor (ITER) is perhaps the greatest co-operative scientific endeavour of our times. Sometime after 2025, and at a cost of around $20 billion, it will be powered up and the scientific world will hold its breath. If it works, the ITER will still produce only five hundred MW of fusion power – far less than the Siemens turbines currently burning gas down there at Didcot B. But the hope is that the lessons learned will lead to large-scale fusion power plants being commissioned in the decades to come.

The standard joke is that fusion power is twenty years in the future and always will be. But according to Tom Barrett, one of Culham's leading engineers: 'We are about to enter the delivery era – fusion is now mainly an engineering problem.' If he is right, and if the scientists here at Culham and their partners around the world can indeed succeed in the truly Promethean endeavour of harnessing the power of fusion, then the Holy Grail of cheap, clean, limitless energy will be within reach.

If the opportunity to attend one of the open evenings at Culham arises, I urge you to go – not only to stare up in wonder at the mundane rivets and bolts of this attempt to harness, here on our planet, the power that drives the sun and stars, but also to witness the passion and the excitement of the young men and women who work there. It is impossible to leave a Culham open evening without shaking the head in wonder and admiration and wishing them all the luck in the world.

&⁓&

Such a brief glance at the past, present and future of our energy supplies, from our vantage point here on the Clumps, may give the impression that the journey to a cleaner future will be a smooth one, carrying us seamlessly from coal to natural gas to wind, solar and fusion power. It won't be like that. Far from Round Hill, the reality is that, even in recent years, new coal-fired power stations have been opening almost every week somewhere in the world. According to the International Energy Agency, coal is responsible for three-quarters of emissions in both China and India – the world's most populous nations. For the United States and the European Union, the dependence on coal is less but still accounts for between a quarter and a third of emissions.

At current usage rates, there is still enough coal in the ground to last an estimated one hundred and fifty years. Add the fact that coal is still the cheapest source of electricity, is easily stockpiled, doesn't need pipelines, sustains hundreds of thousands of jobs and countless companies – and it is clear that coal power is not going to drift peacefully away like the dust of Didcot A's cooling towers.

Sitting here on a clear day overlooking a view of two counties and breathing in the country air, it is strange to think back to a childhood when, every so often, the streets and alleyways would be obscured by the eerie quiet of smog, restricting visibility to three or four paces and conjuring up Jack the Ripper around every corner. Strange, too, to remember flinching at the sight of layers of blue-black scars on an uncle's back as he strip-washed at the kitchen sink – scars embedded with coal dust, caused by roof falls as he sweated by the light of a helmet lamp to jam into place the wooden pit props in the deep and dusty galleries of a Yorkshire coal mine. It all seems like something from the nineteenth century. But all this and worse is still a reality in many parts of the world. Coal is today bringing down the same kind of pollution on Asia's cities that once choked the lungs of Charles Dickens's London. And collapsing galleries and deep mining accidents have been killing an estimated four thousand coal miners every year in China alone.

In remembering all the lives blighted by coal, as well as all the progress and ease it has brought, it is impossible to leave this place without also looking again towards Didcot and thinking of the four men who died even in the process of decommissioning the old coal-fired power plant. On February 23rd, 2016, eighteen months after the great cooling towers had gone, the old boiler house was also being prepared for demolition when it collapsed without warning, burying Christopher Huxtable, Kenneth Cresswell, John Shaw and Michael Collings.

11

Thinking on your Feet

The more you walk the Earth Trust the more you appreciate the variety of these two or three square miles. You have hilltop panoramas and secluded glades, river banks and water meadows, woodlands and wetlands, wildflowers in abundance, and an arboretum of all Oxfordshire's native trees. You don't even need to decide in advance on what kind of walk to take, or where to go, or how far; so many are the intersecting paths that you can always prolong an outing, or cut it short, switch from open hillside to sheltered wood, make for a restful bench, or even head over to nearby Dorchester-on-Thames for a pub lunch or afternoon tea. Underfoot, the going is mostly easy, the tracks broad and grassy, ideal for a side-by-side stroll. But you can also use the two hills, as many fitness groups do, for a tougher work-out.

And so it is that walkers of all kinds are drawn here, strollers to hikers, toddlers to dodderers, trainers and lycra to wellies and tweed. Yet even on fine weekends, when the small car park can quickly fill up, there are rarely more than a few dozen visitors at any one time and these are so quickly dispersed among the many possible trails that you can usually count on being alone within a few minutes of setting out.

What almost all visitors have in common is that they arrive on wheels, walk for a while, and return to their starting point. Nothing remarkable in that, you might think. But in times past it would have seemed an odd thing to do: why expend time and effort only to arrive back where you started from? Today, the answer is obvious: life has become sedentary and walking is the perfect antidote – it's free, always available, suitable for all ages, and comes with a bonus of fresh country air and new horizons.

But as an explanation, this isn't nearly interesting enough: being human, we have to theorise about everything, even something as simple as putting one foot in front of the other. Walking, we are told, helps you to think, lifts your spirits, clears your mind, boosts creativity, and promotes well-being.

Big claims, and with big names attached. Jean-Jacques Rousseau, the father of Romanticism and a hopeless exaggerator said: 'When I stop, I cease to think; my mind only works with my legs.' Montaigne, Kierkegaard, Kant, Hegel, Bentham, Mill – all thought walking an aid to thinking. Nietzsche went as far as to say: 'Do not believe any idea that was not born in the open air.'

Great minds sometimes make daft statements: it is of course perfectly possible to think when sitting down and I suspect it might not be too difficult to compile a list of great ideas born indoors or great philosophers who rarely set foot in the countryside. Possibly, also, there is a mundane explanation for Rousseau's belief that 'there is something about walking which stimulates and enlivens my thoughts,' given that exercise is known to stimulate the flow of oxygen to the brain.

�✍✍

This was the explanation that suggested itself to the Israeli psychologist Daniel Kahneman, who developed many of his own best ideas while walking – leading him to speculate that 'The mild physical arousal of the walk may spill over into greater mental alertness.'

But Kahneman, the only psychologist to win a Nobel Prize in Economics, also noticed something more intriguing. Walking, he observed, seems to help some kinds of thinking and not others.

To test this hypothesis, he recommends a simple experiment: while strolling at a comfortable pace, ask a companion to

multiply twenty-three by seventy-eight. As the mental arith-
metic begins to tick, Kahneman predicts, the pace of walking
will slow. Wondering why this should be, he decided to see what
happened when he approached the problem from the other end
– by increasing the difficulty of the walking rather than the
thinking. Upping his pace to something above four miles per
hour, he became immediately aware of 'a sharp deterioration in
my ability to think coherently'. Again, this is something you can
try for yourself. I have certainly found it to be true, though I
suspect the sharp drop might have been more noticeable in
Kahneman's case. Pushing the enquiry a step further, Kahneman
then tackles a steepish hill while trying to keep up his four-
miles-an-hour. At that point, he finds it difficult to think at all.

At first glance, this seems illogical. Why should hard
walking and hard thinking clash? Surely the one is purely
mental and the other purely physical? And if the two activities
are not drawing on the same resource, why would they come
into conflict?

Kahneman's answer is that certain kinds of physical and
mental exertion do indeed draw on the same resource. The one
may rely primarily on muscle power and the other on brain
power, but both rely on will power. Most of us tend to avoid, if
we can, the strenuous thought involved in complicated calculation or pursuing a rigorous argument to a logical conclusion.
For myself, I greatly admire anyone who, faced with a task
requiring concentrated intellectual effort, does not feel the urge
to investigate the contents of the fridge. But I do not believe
them. Similarly, most of us are tempted to avoid hard physical
exertion, which means that walking uphill at four miles per
hour involves resisting a strong temptation to slow down. And
it is the effort required in overcoming the temptation that
draws on the same limited supply of will power.[13]

If correct, this argument has profound implications which
psychologists have attempted to explore through bizarre exper-

iments. It has been found, for example, that when asked to undertake demanding mental tasks at the same time as being given the choice of chocolate cake or fruit salad, people are more likely to choose the chocolate cake. The reason, apparently, is that performing the mental task is drawing on some of the will power needed to choose the healthier option. In four decades of studying this question, the Australian psychologist Roy Baumeister has shown repeatedly that all kinds of difficult voluntary effort – whether physical, cognitive or emotional – draw in part on the same limited pool of mental energy. As does coping with stress, which can make demands on all of these different kinds of effort at the same time.

All this might help to explain why people are often able to stick to a diet or an exercise regime when life is going well, only to relapse when the stresses and demands start to build up. Keeping up a good resolution requires just that – resolution. And it suggests that the reason that the poor, on average, tend to smoke more and eat more than the middle classes is not that they have less will power but because the stresses and demands of coping with poverty are a constant drain on the power of resolution.

∼∽

If this argument helps to explain why hard thinking and hard walking do not go well together, it still leaves the question of why walking seems to be a positive help to so many novelists, essayists, poets and philosophers.

Given that it is not the rigorous A-to-B kind of thinking that is helped, it must be another kind: the more free-wheeling, non-linear kind that we are perhaps all more familiar with. As if to confirm the idea, the very language we use to describe this kind of thinking seems to suggest walking: our thoughts 'ramble' or 'wander' or 'stray' or 'go round in circles' or, more positively, help us 'get things in perspective' or 'see things from a different point of view'.

But although this constant supply of metaphor from walking to thinking suggests that the two activities might in some way be complementary, mind and body rambling along together, it still does not explain why walking should be such a positive advantage. So perhaps there is some insight to be gained by Kahneman's method of looking at the question from the other end and asking 'what are the disadvantages of attempting this kind of thinking indoors?'

Thoughts may, of course, wander from deep within an armchair. But the view does not change a great deal, and so the stimulus to thinking comes mainly from inside one's own head, which can be a stultifying place to be. Perhaps, also, thinking while slumped in a chair conveys the impression, to oneself and others, that one is doing nothing, so inducing a mild feeling of guilt. Walking in the fresh air, by contrast, is doing something, and may even induce a mild feeling of virtue.

Probably more to the point, to be indoors is to be aware of the ever-present possibility of doing something else. Every home is fully furnished with things you ought to do be doing. Every footstep or opening door, every ring of the phone or ping of an app, every glimpse of screen or in-tray or undone task, brings on an assault of musts and shoulds and oughts. And if this mild barrage of obligation and responsibility becomes a little oppressive, and if the concentration on the task in hand is proving a little arduous, then why not see what's happening in the news, delete a few emails, click on a promising link, check if one's friends have posted anything interesting, or decide that it's time for a light snack? Amazing, really, that any thinking at all gets done indoors.

All this vanishes as you step out on to the Clumps. To walk in the countryside is to clear the decks of domesticity and obligation. It is truly to let the mind off the leash and allow thought to wander where it will. Any stray association prompted by the ever-changing view can be pursued. Every spontaneous thought, every unconnected notion, every diversion and non-sequitur, can come and go without the need to make confession or impose a restraining order. To writers, in particular, this may be the great advantage – permitting randomness full play, allowing new thoughts to arise unchecked, opening up space for new ideas to breathe and creativity come into its own.

As this implies, the appeal of walking seems to lie partly in walking *away*. Thoreau said that what walking gave him was the freedom to think 'without being invaded by volatile, deafening hassles or alienated by the incessant cackle of chatterers'. Incidentally, it also allowed him to escape 'the news' which in Thoreau's time had become a kind of craze made possible by the telegraph. 'After a night's sleep,' he wrote, 'the news has become as indispensable as the breakfast … hardly a man takes a half-hour's nap after dinner but when he wakes he holds up his head and asks – What's the news?' Thoreau's cure for this addictive treadmill of trivia driven by 'wanting to know what happens next' was to replace the daily newspaper with a daily walk. Not hard to imagine, then, what he would have thought about a twenty-four-hour news cycle streamed to mobile phones.

More recently, the philosopher Frederic Gross has developed this idea that the appeal of walking, especially for writers, is the appeal of walking away. Works written in libraries and studies, he believes, are weighted down by citations and the words of other authors, while works composed while walking outdoors are free to soar without the trappings of other minds. Known in his native France as the 'Professor of Walking', Gross also believes that walking offers a more fundamental kind of escape, allowing the mind to escape from reputation and social expectations and even from one's own identity. The freedom of walking, he argues, is freedom from one's own past, so that when walking you are 'just an eddy in the immemorial stream of life'.

If all this seems just a tiny bit French and fanciful, and if eddying in the immemorial stream of life doesn't sound much like walking on the Wittenham Clumps, then perhaps it's time to conclude with the more down-to-earth approach of the most famous of all 'walking writers'.

For William Wordsworth, writing and walking were almost inseparable. Many of his poems were composed as he walked the fells of Grasmere or Ullswater, often mumbling lines to himself over and over, getting the rhythm right and occasionally stopping to scribble down a line that satisfied him. A gardener at Rydal Mount in the Lake District has left us this marvellous description of the process:

> 'He would set his head a bit forrad, and put his hands
> behint his back. And then he would start a bumming,
> and it was bum, bum, bum, stop; then bum, bum, reet
> down till t'other end; and then he'd set down and git a
> bit o'paper and write a bit.'

The 'bumming' is perhaps another clue to the link between writing and walking. Second only to the breath and the pulse, walking sets up the most common and natural rhythm of our lives – our 'natural andante' as David Malouf described it. And it is probably because of the steady rhythm of walking, and its age-old use as a way of pacing out and measuring length, that the Greeks used the word 'foot' to describe the basic unit of rhythm in poetic metre. Lines of poetry could then be divided up into 'feet' as a way of identifying and describing different rhythmical patterns or 'metre'. They gave the name 'iamb' to a foot consisting of an unstressed syllable followed by a stressed syllable – for example, 'to*day*'. The reverse pattern, stressed syllable followed by unstressed syllable – '*daily*' – they called a 'trochee'. There are other kinds of 'feet', but the great majority of English poets through the ages have chosen to write in iambic metre (specifically in iambic pentameter, in which each line is made up of five iambs). This is the metre of all of Shakespeare's plays, and most English poetry from the Elizabethans through the Romantics to the First World War. And it has given us some of our most famous lines:

> *If music be the food of love, play on* – Shakespeare
>
> *Season of mists and mellow fruitfulness*[14] – Keats
>
> *Our sweetest songs are those of saddest thought* – Shelley
>
> *If I should die, think only this of me* – Brooke

The wonderful thing about iambic poetry is that it never strays far from the rhythms of ordinary, everyday speech. The term 'iambic pentameter' may sound arcane, but it can be heard on a bus or a street corner:

> *I think the car has hit a concrete post*
>
> *So cheap the queue went right around the block*
>
> *I'd like a drink but then my head would ache*
>
> *I walked as far as Wittenham Clumps and back*

All of these are lines of iambic pentameter. Or, to take an example from iambic tetrameter (four iambs per line), 'I wandered lonely as a cloud' has the same rhythmical pattern as 'I like my coffee nice and strong'.

This closeness to everyday speech means that an iambic line, on its own, may appear to have no special poetic quality. But when run together, line after line, repeated iambic 'feet' set up the recognisable rhythmical pattern that is one of the elements that helps make poetry powerful, memorable, and a pleasure to listen to. The pattern of expectation can be and often is broken to great effect, but by staying within touching distance of the rhythms of everyday speech, iambic metre has long helped prevent English poetry from becoming too stilted and high flown.

Wordsworth, especially in his younger days, was passionately committed to this idea that poetry should not be too different from everyday language. Verse was different from speech, he believed, mainly because of its sustained rhythmical pattern. And it seems likely that the description of the poet 'bum, bum, bumming' as he walked means that he was using the rhythm of his walk as a kind of metronome for his composing. The language, for the most part, remains close to speech, but the rhythm is a two-hundred-year echo of the poet's footsteps. And his long walks gave him not only an outing 'In which the heavy and the weary weight of all this unintelligible world is lightened,' but also helped him express that feeling in iambic pentameter.

The rhythm of a Wordsworth poem – 'a two-hundred-year echo of the poet's footsteps'
(Image: Wikimedia Commons)

అంశం

I find I am reluctant to close this ramble on rambling without at least trying to add something about another aspect of walking that is so vague and intangible as to be difficult to put into any kind of words. Thoreau had a try at it when he wrote that walking 'magnifies receptiveness: I am always receiving pure presence by the ton.'

I know what he means, even if he does make it sound like receiving a delivery of coal.

Frederic Gross, our 'Professor of Walking', also tries to describe the feeling when he writes that 'walking can help the walker to experience 'the fullness of feeling alive' and 'the joy of living, of feeling oneself here'. But he also believes this feeling is best left to poetry rather than prose. And so, ludicrous as it may be to move swiftly and without pause from Wordsworth to my own amateur toe in the waters of verse, I will conclude with a poem drafted on the Wittenham Clumps.

The reader who is paying attention will notice that, unlike an earlier poem in this volume (Chapter *A layer of woollen air*), the lines below are written in the 'free verse'. As opposed to metrical poetry, free verse does not feel obliged to conform to any regular or predictable rhythmical pattern. Indeed, its harsher critics have said it is so ill-defined and undisciplined that it opens the way for anyone to write some prose, chop it into short lines, and call it poetry. More wittily, the American poet Robert Frost has described free verse as 'like playing tennis without a net'.

Wordsworth, of course, would not have approved and would no doubt have recommended re-writing the poem to the rhythm of my footsteps rather than sitting on a bench at the top of Round Hill. But as readers will notice, not unkindly I hope, I am no Wordsworth.

A damp place in a wood

Who has not stopped by a damp place in a wood,
startled by ordinariness, by breath, by blood,
by the touch of day on hands and face,
by the anonymity of a leaf,
by the weight of the world underfoot?

Of course it cannot last, this moment of
uncounted time, this old eternity
in the missed beat of earth, like a new tense,
future infinitive, future forgotten,
the time that never was and always was.

And then the heart-stopped world returns
and the plain stare of ordinary is ordinary again.
And yet the moment surely stood
for something, and stands for something still,
by this damp place in a wood

where mist is handing day to evening,
ghosting the trees, curtaining the vision
to nearer margins, closer kindnesses,
whose modest colours, innocent of glare,
now come into their own, and fineness fills the air.

12

Beware of the Yellow Waistcoat

The Earth Trust, which owns the Wittenham Clumps and much of the land around, is said to welcome one hundred and fifty thousand people a year, making it Oxfordshire's most-visited outdoor attraction. Strange, for a place that seems to offer so much solitude.

Then I remembered a statistician friend, a demographer, who when informed that a small African country was importing five million condoms a year replied that this statistic was useful for tracking overall demand, but didn't tell us whether it meant five million men using one condom a year, or one man using five million a year. Is it possible, I wondered, that the Earth Trust visitor total might be susceptible to the same statistical weakness? After all, one hundred and fifty thousand visits a year could mean one hundred and fifty thousand people visiting once a year, or just over four hundred people visiting once a day. Given that most of the people I regularly see on the Clumps are daily dog walkers, the second interpretation seems likely to be closer to the mark.

It would not be quite true to say that I haven't any interest in dogs. I have always been slightly interested in how that red-in-tooth-and-claw carnivore, the savage wolf that hunts in packs and haunts the forests of fairy-tales, managed to get itself re-branded as 'man's best friend'. As I say, slightly interested. Not enough to find out.

This changed when I happened to be looking through a brochure for the Oxford Literary Festival. One of the talks on offer was by a geneticist who had written a book about how, when, where and why wolves became dogs. And so it was that I found myself taking a seat, along with about a hundred others, in the modern, steeply raked lecture theatre of the Weston Library, waiting to have my slight interest satisfied with the minimum of effort on my part.

I should have realised that things were not going to go well when the lecturer appeared on the podium wearing yellow trousers and a matching waistcoat. There is no excuse for this kind of thing, even in Oxford, but I set aside my prejudices and waited patiently for the talk to begin.

Following good academic practice of full disclosure, the speaker started by clarifying his own relationship with dogs – 'They don't like me and I don't like them ... they have always seemed to me to be malodorous spongers.' Wasn't it then a bit odd to choose to write a book about them? Not at all, said the author, answering his own question: if you had to like the subject of your books no one would ever have written a biography of Stalin.

There have been some wonderful lectures at the Oxford Literary Festival over the years, but it soon became clear that this was not going to be one of them. Suffice it to say that I left the Weston Library an hour later, £12.50 lighter and very little wiser.

&♥&

There is perhaps no greater measure of human progress than the transition from lapdogs to laptops and within half an hour, from the comfort of my own home, I was able to assemble an international panel of experts to provide me with a much better explanation of why ninety per cent of walkers on the Wittenham Clumps are being towed along by the descendants of wolves.

The first step on that journey is not in dispute. Darwin lamented that 'we shall never be able to ascertain the origin of dogs with certainty' and wondered whether perhaps jackals and hyenas might have been part of the pedigree. But fast forward to the present day and we have indeed ascertained it with certainty: in 2005, the sequencing of the dog genome revealed that all of today's dogs are descended from a single species of grey wolf, now extinct.

Much less certain is the where, when and why of wolves becoming dogs, though teams of scientists at half a dozen universities around the world are closing in on the answers. From analysis of DNA from prehistoric dog bones, some say that the domestication of the wolf happened only once, somewhere in Asia. Others believe it also happened independently somewhere in Europe. But what is known for certain is that wolf-dogs were the first animals to be domesticated by humans and that it happened somewhere between twenty and forty thousand years ago. This means that dogs became part of our lives long before the growing of crops or the keeping of cattle. 'Domesticating the wolf,' says Brian Hare, Director of the Duke University Canine Cognition Center, 'was one of the most extraordinary events in human history.' And it was extraordinary because it meant that humans had, for the first time, enlisted the help of another species in the struggle for survival, initially for hunting and later for purposes as diverse as guarding sheep and dragging sleds across the ice.

Why and how this step in our own evolution happened has been much debated (you are entitled to stop reading if I use the expression 'bone of contention'). One theory is that our relationship with dogs must have started with some distant ancestor befriending an injured wolf. But the experts are sniffy about this. 'Anyone who has spent time with wild wolves,' says Hare, 'would see how unlikely it was that we somehow tamed them in a way that led to domestication.'

A more plausible explanation might seem to be the adoption of an abandoned wolf cub by a soft-hearted cave-dweller. But modern attempts to tame wolf cubs from birth suggest that it is all but impossible for domestication to have happened this way. Even abandoned fox cubs cannot be made into pets.[15]

No, the explanation that commands the support of most experts is that wolves became dogs by 'selecting for tameness' over several generations – a process that probably came about by wolves choosing humans rather than the other way around. Natural variation, the theory goes, would have meant that some wolves were less fearful of humans than others, enabling them to take advantage of the bones and scraps of food lying around hunter-gatherer settlements. This additional source of food gave them a survival edge and so 'propensity to friendliness towards humans' began to exert a selective evolutionary pressure. In other words, we did not tame dogs; dogs tamed themselves.

A good theory is always helped by a good story, and in this case we are lucky to have the touching tale of Dmitri and the Fox Factory.

The story begins in the 1950s when Russian scientist Dmitry Belyaev and a young intern, Lyudmila Trut, started a project to try to find out how animals had first become domesticated. Unfortunately, Stalin had banned genetic research in the Soviet Union, believing the whole idea of genetic inheritance to be counter-revolutionary. So Belyaev and Trut had to pretend that the aim of their research was to improve the quality of Russian fox furs, and it was in this guise that they began visiting fox farms from Siberia to Estonia. On each farm, they observed what happened when they first entered the foxes' cages: any animal that seemed markedly less fearful and aggressive was selected for transportation to Belyaev's own fox farm in Novosibirsk, three and a half thousand kilometres east of

Lyudmila Trut (1933–), Russian geneticist, ethologist, and evolutionist whose lifetime work sought to reproduce what natural evolution had achieved over thousands of years. *(Photograph: Vasily Koval, 2012, Creative Commons, Share Alike 4.0).*

Moscow. Eventually, one hundred vixens and thirty male foxes were installed as the first generation of parents in the great domestication experiment.

Belyaev and Trut then repeated the process, selecting the tamest ten per cent of each new litter of cubs to become the next generation of parents (while the other ninety per cent were sold off to be made into fur coats). Admittedly this friend-or-fur offer may seem a little mafia-like, but it seems to have been an effective selection pressure. Only three generations later, the Novosibirsk fox cubs were lacking almost all signs of fear or aggression. By the sixth generation, a small percentage were seeking human company. By the tenth generation, half of them were well on their way to being 'man's best friend'.

During all of the experiments at Novosibirsk, there was little contact between the caged foxes and the researchers: domestication was achieved solely by selective breeding. Through enforcing the 'survival of the friendliest', Belyaev and Trut reproduced the same process as natural evolution had achieved over thousands of years – and with the same results.

But also with some unexpected results. Breeding for 'friendliness' is genetic modification. And in dogs, as in humans, it is almost impossible to modify just one section of the genome without affecting others. In the case of the Novosibirsk foxes, the researchers were surprised to find that, as they became tamer, so ears started to flop, tails to wag, and markings to change. Summing up these unexpected developments, one researcher commented that, scientifically speaking, the animals had become 'even more adorable'. Much later, and far from Novosibirsk, it was also discovered that the part of the genome affected by domestication is linked with Williams-Beuren syndrome – a genetic disorder in humans with consequences that can include over-trusting behaviours.

When wolves began to change by this same evolutionary process, happening naturally over thousands of years, it seems that as they became more trusting and floppier about the ears they also began to lose the ability to work in packs. Instead, they learnt to read social cues and cooperate with humans. Laurie Santos, Director of Yale University's Canine Cognition Center, set up an experiment in which food was only accessible by solving an impossible puzzle – involving box lids that wouldn't open and levers that wouldn't pull. Wolves tried everything and kept on trying; dogs gave up after a minute or two and looked appealingly to the nearest human.

❧

This leads me to the only other question about dogs that has stirred a faint interest as I have said 'good morning' to many hundreds of dog walkers on the Wittenham Clumps. It seems perfectly plausible that the Alsatian straining powerfully at the leash is descended from a wolf. But that little chihuahua racing alongside its strolling owner? Or that Dalmatian being stared down by stoical Hereford cattle? Or the Dachshund having its belly tickled by the grass in Church Meadow? Or the Great Dane striding handsomely through Little Wittenham Wood? No other species in the world has as much variety in size, shape or temperament as the dog. And especially not us. There is only one species of dog, just as there is only one species of human. But compared to dogs, members of the human species are practically identical.

The first part of the answer is easy enough. All of today's dog breeds are the result of human selection. And just as wolves became dogs through thousands of years of selecting for tameness, so dogs became breeds through thousands of years of selecting for characteristics such as how much help they were in the hunt, or how reliable they were as guard dogs, or how much stamina they had for pulling sleds, or how docile they were as companions. It is a process that continues to this day in the selecting and breeding of dogs for specific abilities like sniffing out drugs or helping the visually impaired.

A few breeds of dog have been our companions for millennia. Greyhounds are depicted on four-thousand-year-old Egyptian vases. Siberian Huskies go back at least nine thousand years. But the great majority of today's breeds are newcomers, unknown as recently as two hundred years ago. Some have been bred for practical tasks; others for being cute or fashionable.

If this had stopped at some sensible point, then there would perhaps be little wrong with selectively breeding dogs to be good companions, to be loving, friendly, docile, or good with children. Some of these more appealing qualities have certainly been developed, and dogs even seem to have taken advantage by hacking into the human bonding process. Laurie Santos's research shows that when a dog and human share a loving gaze, both brains secrete oxytocin – the hormone linked to both trust and maternal bonding.

Unfortunately, the sillier side of human nature has also taken a hand. And it was the Victorians who started it all by extending their snobbish notions of aristocracy, 'blue blood' and good breeding into the innocent world of dogs. The Kennel Club was formed in London in 1873 and has since bred imitators in over a hundred countries. It is the officials of such clubs who decide what the ideal 'look' of each breed should be, keeping records of parentage and pedigree in a kind of canine Burke's Peerage. A 'pure-bred' dog means nothing more than both parents being known to be of the same breed and with the right 'look'.

Unfortunately, it's easy to breed dogs if you're not too concerned about researching an animal's family history and health. Find two dogs with especially curly eyebrows, encourage them to mate, and in a generation or two you'll likely have a new breed of pure-bred Curlywurlies. Helped by dog shows and 'best of breed' competitions, commercial breeders began supplying dogs that conformed to 'the look' or were unusual, or rare, or owned by celebrities. In recent years, for example, designer cross-breeds have become the 'dog to be seen with'. The Cockapoo – a cross between a cocker spaniel and poodle – is now being marketed by breeders for around £3,000 a pup.

≈≈≈

It might be assumed that all this is silly but harmless. Not so. Breeding from a narrow and artificially restricted genetic pool increases the likelihood of pups being born with genetic defects. The ideal pug, for example, must have those beady eyes that carry an increased risk of eye disease and blindness (as do the endearing 'droopy eyes' of bloodhounds). The standard for the ideal English bulldog includes a short muzzle in a flattened face, but this is often associated with breathing problems. Tea-cup poodles and other dogs bred for an unnatural smallness are prone to fragile bones and dislocated knees. At the other extreme, unnatural largeness brings an increased risk of leg tumours. Dalmatians are susceptible to deafness; Boxers to heart conditions, arthritis, cancers, breathing problems, epilepsy and eye problems. Breeding dogs with similar genetic characteristics is also quicker and easier if you are prepared to in-breed them, say with their close cousins. Among human populations, in-breeding is illegal almost everywhere because of the increased genetic risk. For dogs, the risk is the same, but the law is not. And this opens the door for the so-called 'puppy mills' that turn out litters of dogs in response to changing fashions in a manner that more closely resembles the production line of a sweat-shop fashion factory. In the worst cases, female dogs are made to breed too young and too often and, when exhausted, are cast out to fend for themselves.

So, on the one hand, we have millions being spent on 'pure-bred' puppies in the mistaken belief that they are somehow superior. And on the other we have animal shelters filling up with abandoned dogs, a high proportion of which are 'pure-breds' and many of which have to be put down because the shelters cannot cope. In the United States, about seventy million pets are abandoned each year, of which animal shelters can take in about one in ten. Of the rest, more than a million are put down. In our own nation of animal-lovers, according to a report by the BBC, fifty thousand dogs a year are abandoned, of which about five thousand are put down. None of this is on display at Crufts.

Oh dear, this was going to be such a light-hearted chapter raising nothing more distressing than the dress sense of Oxford academics. But instead, I seem to have wandered off the Clumps into a dark world of genetic defects and greedy breeders, if you'll forgive the expression. And I'm afraid that even the story of Dmitry and the Fox Factory does not have a happy ending. The experimental farm at Novosibirsk struggles on to this day under the direction of that same young intern of the 1950s, Lyudmila Trut, now aged eighty-eight. To help ease financial pressures, a small number of domesticated foxes were offered for sale as pets to wealthy Americans seeking 'something a little different'. The first to make the trip – a red fox named Anya – was bought for $9,000 by a Kay Fedewa who, after much paperwork, succeeded in importing the animal and housing it in a specially built compound in the garden of her home in Michigan. This, too, might have seemed silly but harmless. After all, from the fox's point of view, defecting to America might seem the better option if close contact with humans came down to a choice between being a pampered pet in Michigan or a fur coat in Kazakhstan. Unfortunately, when Anya arrived in her new home, Ms Fedewa's inadequate fencing and Anya's trusting nature led her to cosy up to a coyote that tore off her leg and left her to bleed to death.

To end on a happier note, the dog walkers of the Wittenham Clumps seem a far more sensible lot than those to be found at Crufts or the National Dog Show. Nor do the dogs on Round and Fort Hill appear to be genetic freaks. On the contrary, it seems obvious that all these daily rain-or-shine outings on the Clumps contribute enormously not only to the Earth Trust's statistical visitor tally but to the overall health and well-being of those on both ends of the leash.

13

OF HEDGEROWS AND HEDGE FUNDS

Ask a companion to point out the salient features of the view from the Wittenham Clumps and the chances are he or she will probably not mention one of the most obvious.

So taken for granted are hedgerows that they seem a natural part of the landscape. But at the time the Clumps were first planted, most of these hedgerows would have seemed anything but natural. They were a means and a symbol of oppression. And they were bitterly resented.

The pain and turmoil that followed the eighteenth-century Enclosure Acts has long settled into the dust of history. What remains are these quiet lines of hawthorn and hazel with the occasional spindle or guelder rose. Many have been torn out in recent times to make way for ever-larger farm machines. But those that remain are a memorial to an upheaval that transformed society.

The eighteenth-century landowners who planted these hedges may be remembered today for their ha-has and picturesque clumps of trees, but their real business was driving up yields and profits by means of the new agricultural techniques. And that meant putting an end to the old system of the commons and individual strips of farmland, each one growing the plants and crops that made a family more or less self-sufficient.

With larger fields, new techniques like seed drilling and crop rotation could be brought to bear on the land, so that there was no need to let a third of the land lie fallow. As for the traditional commons, the selective breeding of cattle, sheep or pigs was only possible if livestock could be prevented from mingling and breeding freely. The answer was to petition Parliament for an Act of Enclosure that allowed whoever owned the land to close off the commons with fences and hedges. As a rule of thumb, hedges that run in straight lines are likely to date from the time of the Enclosures; those that follow a more eccentric course are likely to be older.

In the century when the Wittenham Clumps were growing to maturity, more than four thousand Enclosure Acts passed through Parliament, closing off common lands equivalent to about a sixth of the area of England. In the villages we can see from the Clumps, Enclosure came to Aston Tirrold in 1743 and 1808, Upton in 1758, Aston Upthorpe in 1793 and 1808, Harwell in 1802, and Brightwell in 1809. Until 1812, for example, the parish of Long Wittenham had very few defined fields, just the great open spaces known, since Norman times as North Field and West Field. But under pressure from landowners like the Prowses and the Lovegroves, and the Fellows of Exeter College, Oxford, they were divided up and fenced or hedged to make fields with names like Lark Furlong, Middle Furlong, Great Furlong, Deep Furrow, or Walnut Tree Piece.

The result of all this upheaval was that yields almost doubled over the course of the eighteenth century. But a change that meant more profit for landowners meant more poverty for smallholders, tenant farmers and landless labourers. Since mediaeval times, they had been relatively secure in their traditional rights to the commons on which they might keep a few geese or chickens, or graze a cow, or cut turf, or grow vegetables, or gather fruits, herbs and firewood. A Parliamentary Enclosure Act over-rode all such rights, no matter that a cow's milk and a few eggs a week could make the difference between self-sufficiency and destitution.

This, in essence, is what lay behind the long conflict that is represented by the peaceful hedgerows that we see from the

Clumps today, dividing up the meadows by the Thames and the fields that stretch southwards to the Berkshire Downs.

≪୬≫

The conflict was long and bitter. But it was an unequal contest from the start. Landowners had little difficulty in having Enclosure Acts passed by a Parliament made up almost entirely of landowners like themselves. Even when challenged in the local courts, where customary rights were difficult to prove, the decision almost invariably went in favour of the landowner, not least because to be a Justice of the Peace you had to be – you guessed it – a landowner. In some cases, a miserly compensation was paid. In nearby Hadden (now the Hadden Hill Golf Course), two dozen poor villagers were instructed that their rights to collect wood for winter fuel had been withdrawn; the landowner, Brasenose College, Oxford, offered instead ten pounds worth of coal to be distributed each Christmas. Often, there was no compensation at all. According to E. P. Thompson, author of the classic *The Making of the English Working Class*, the Enclosure Acts were 'not much more than an act of theft'.

It might be thought that the church would have had something to say about all this. After all, the rural parson was an influential figure and could perhaps have been expected to have some sympathy for the poor. But rents on land and tithes on yields provided much of the income for many rural clergymen, and as the yield and value of land increased so their incomes swelled. The country clergy were, in any case, unlikely to rock the establishment boat, being appointed for the most part by the local Lord of the Manor or noble family. So rather than taking up the cause of the poor and the dispossessed, many of the clergy sided with their patrons, practising a cold charity in the parish and preaching acquiescence on Sundays. There were of course honourable exceptions, but the church's position is perhaps best summed up in the third verse of that ever-popular hymn 'All Things Bright and Beautiful':

> *The rich man in his castle,*
> *The poor man at his gate,*
> *God made them high and lowly,*
> *And ordered their estate.*

∾

If the parsons did not speak for the poor, the poets did their best.

Oliver Goldsmith, son and grandson of Anglican clergymen, wrote his most famous poem – 'The Deserted Village' – as a protest against what was happening to the English – countryside during these years. One couplet sums up the message:

> *Those fenceless fields the sons of wealth divide,*
> *And even the bare-worn common is denied.*

In particular, he poured poetic scorn on landowners who evicted the poor to create fashionable landscaped grounds with

> *Space for his lake, his park's extended bounds,*
> *Space for his horses, equipage, and hounds.*

'The Deserted Village' was written after Goldsmith witnessed an actual village being demolished to make way for landscaping an aristocrat's estate. In the poem, the village was given the name 'Sweet Auburn', and Goldsmith never revealed the name of the real village on which it was based. But he did leave clues. It is known, for example, that it was about fifty miles from London, and that the poet witnessed its destruction in the year 1761. That makes it probable that the real 'deserted village' was Nuneham Courtenay, about three miles north of the Wittenham Clumps, which was demolished in 1761 to make way for the landscaping of the Earl Harcourt's country estate. The villagers were relocated about a mile and a half away in the brick semi-detached cottages that now face each other on either side of the A4074 Oxford-to-Henley road.

More than anything else, 'The Deserted Village' was a protest at the destruction of Britain's 'bold peasantry' in the name of trade and profit. And like many poets before and since, there was more than a dash of sentimentality in Goldsmith's ideas about the rural poor. In contrast to the present when 'One only master grasps the whole domain,' the poem portrays the past as a rural idyll:

> A time there was, ere England's griefs began,
> When every rood of ground maintained its man;
> For him light labour spread her wholesome store,
> Just gave what life required, but gave no more:
> His best companions, innocence and health;
> And his best riches, ignorance of wealth.
>
> But times are altered; trade's unfeeling train
> Usurp the land and dispossess the swain.

Written at the height of the Enclosure movement, Goldsmith's poem also provided the couplet that has been quoted ever since by protesters against economic injustice:

> Ill fares the land, to hastening ills a prey,
> Where wealth accumulates, and men decay.

It was all to no avail. Sixty years later, John Clare, the 'peasant poet' was still raising a forlorn flag of dissent as thousands of Enclosure Acts continued to leave the countryside 'beset wi' posts and rails and turnēd upside down.' Clare even compared the Acts to the devastation inflicted on Europe by Napoleon: 'Enclosure like a Bonaparte let not a thing remain.'

A more obscure poet, known to those familiar with the Wittenham Clumps, showed his solidarity with the poor in a quite different way. Joseph Tubb of Warborough, author of the lines carved into the 'Poem Tree' on Fort Hill, spent time in Oxford jail for protesting a local Enclosure Act by tearing down fences.

છુબ્જ

All in all, the Enclosure movement had the profound effect of consolidating a class system in which ownership of land largely determined status in society. Almost as much as 'good blood', it was the possession of a landed estate that conferred rank and respectability. Even those whose wealth had come via trade bought into the ethos, knowing that a generation or two of landowning could lift them into the gentry. Land was what decided which families you could call upon, dine with, or marry into. And land was what qualified you and your sons for positions of influence in the church, the military, the courts or Parliament. In short, as Karl Marx never tired of arguing, it was the Enclosure Acts that transformed the feudal system into the class system.

Thanks to Jane Austen, who delicately delineated and relentlessly satirised its absurdities, the class system of the eighteenth and nineteenth centuries needs no description here (it is a myth that the British are more obsessed by class than other countries – it is just that we are better at making television series about it).

છુબ્જ

All of this economic and social history is hinted at by the miles of hedgerows seen from this, or almost any other hilltop in the

English landscape. But as I sit here on Round Hill thinking about hedges and fences, I am reminded, as I have been many times over the years, of something I learnt a long time ago, and in a place very far from the Wittenham Clumps.

It was in the 1970s, and I was in New Delhi to write about the Green Revolution that was doubling and trebling the yields of the Punjab. Talking with Norman Borlaug, the Nobel Prize-winning plant scientist known as 'the father of the green revolution', it was hard not to share his enthusiasm for what was an extraordinary scientific breakthrough. But later, when talking to farmers in the countryside, the picture was more muddied.

What was happening, in essence, was this: the government in Delhi had begun to promote the new strains of 'miracle wheat' by training agricultural extension workers to bring the good news to the nation's farmers. When they called on the larger landowners to introduce the new varieties of seed, they were generally welcomed. Wealthier farmers were at ease with officialdom and could ask questions and read the literature. They could also afford the inputs of pesticides and fertiliser on which the miracle depended. Even more important, they could afford to risk a few acres to try out the new seeds. Then, when yields did indeed double or treble, they put hundreds more acres under the 'miracle seeds' and harvests and profits boomed.

Down the road, the agricultural extension workers found their task both more difficult and less congenial. Often the small farmers were suspicious of officialdom, could not read the literature left behind, and could not afford the fertiliser and pesticides. They were also wary of seed that had to be bought with cash each year, rather than being kept back from last year's harvest. Probably most important of all, they could not afford to take a risk when an acre or two was all the land they had and failure might mean starvation or bankruptcy. Thanks, but no thanks, we'll stay with what we know.

The following year, when the output from the larger landholdings doubled, the grain flowed into the silos and the price at market fell. The small farmer now received much less for his or her small surplus, which meant a struggle to afford basics like rent or kerosene or schoolbooks. The alternative was to borrow, and the readiest source of a loan was usually the local landowner who was looking to invest his new profits in loans or more land in order to sow even more acres with the new variety of seed. When the same thing happened in the following years and mounting debts could not be repaid, the landlord might graciously accept land in payment of the debt. In this way, the surpluses and the landholdings of the larger farmers continued to increase, while the ranks of the indebted and the landless swelled.

I think what has brought this story to mind so many times over the years is that it represents a clear example of a recurring pattern, a truth that could be illustrated by a thousand examples. Whether in England in 1770 or India in 1970, the introduction of new technologies into unequal societies has a tendency to widen existing inequalities. It is a story at least as old as Matthew 25:29: 'For unto every one that hath shall be given, and he shall have abundance: but from him that hath not, shall be taken away even that which he hath.'

This is not a Luddite argument, or a sentimental lament for the past, or a protest against modernisation and progress. The Green Revolution eventually meant that hundreds of millions of families in India's towns and cities could afford to feed themselves, and has helped give India an unprecedented seventy years without a major famine. Similarly in Britain, the Enclosure Acts and the agricultural revolution of the eighteenth century dramatically increased the yield of the land, making it possible to feed a rapidly growing urban and industrial population. John Clare may have seen the Enclosure movement as a threat similar to that posed by Napoleon, but without it Napoleon's Continental

System might well have succeeded in its aim of starving out Britain in the early years of the nineteenth century.

So the point is not to decry modernisation but to argue that transition to the new – whether from traditional seeds to miracle wheat, or from common lands to enclosed fields, or from struggling coal mines to industries with a future, or from assembly lines and office work to robots and artificial intelligence – follows a trajectory which leads to widening inequality and comes at a price that falls most heavily on those least able to bear it.

In essence, this pattern is neither complex nor surprising. In a free market system, the benefits of new methods and technologies will inevitably accrue first and foremost to those who are best placed to take advantage of them. In our own time, we may be witnessing the most dramatic example of all as the surge of technological and digital innovation creates global markets and new industries that lift millions out of poverty, but also creates vast new inequalities and devastates the lives and the communities of those who are left behind.

Having come this far, I am obliged to nail political colours to the mast. I am not a socialist in the sense of believing in state ownership of the means of production or state control of every service that a modern society needs. I believe that a combination of free enterprise and democratic government, for all its failings, is the best arrangement for promoting and safeguarding the common good. But if that arrangement is to work then it should also be acknowledged that unrestrained market forces have an inbuilt dynamic towards increasing inequality, and that it is a prime responsibility of government to act as a counterweight to this tendency. As much as ensuring its citizens' safety and upholding the rule of law, it is the task of government in a civilised society to offset the momentum towards inequality, to safeguard social cohesion, and to protect those disadvantaged by innovation.

Whether this happens or not depends on enterprise and law being subject to democratic control. Only this, in the end, can ensure that the legal and fiscal framework within which the market operates is organised in the interests of society as a whole. The obvious threat to that democratic control is that those who benefit disproportionately from technological and economic advance – whether they be eighteenth-century landowners or twenty-first-century hedge fund managers – usually find ways to translate that advantage into political influence. When this is allowed to happen, as it has already happened to such an extreme degree in the United States, it feeds into a spiral by which increasing concentration of wealth at the top translates into increasing influence over the political process, which in turn results in the kind of fiscal and regulatory changes which tilt the playing field ever further in favour of the advantaged. In short, when democratic control is corroded by allowing wealth to translate into greater political influence for the rich, then government becomes not a counterweight to growing inequality but an additional cause.

So it seems appropriate to close with a less well-known stanza of 'The Deserted Village', in which Goldsmith makes an ironic appeal to politicians to do something to prevent inequality from growing to the point of excess on one side and misery on the other:

> *Ye friends to truth, ye statesmen, who survey*
> *The rich man's joys increase, the poor's decay,*
> *'Tis yours to judge how wide the limits stand*
> *Between a splendid and a happy land.*

Now, what was I talking about? Oh yes, hedgerows …

III

THE POINT OF DAFFODILS

Illustration: Sarah Woolfenden

You normally have to be bashed about a bit by life to see the point of daffodils, sunsets and uneventful nice days.

Alain de Botton

14

PETAL POWER

I first began to look at wildflowers while walking on the Wittenham Clumps, idly observing the changes brought by the passing seasons. Gradually, I learned some of their names and downloaded images of the more common flowers to make an old-fashioned 'I spy' book for my granddaughters, so they could rush about on the Clumps disturbing the peace with their shouts of recognition.

In spring and summer, to walk on Fort Hill is to be accompanied every step of the way by cheering crowds of wildflowers. There are dog roses and primroses, rock rose and cowslip, poppies and harebells, melilot and yellow rattle, cranesbill and storksbill, restharrow and wild marjoram, and sometimes whole acres of bright ox-eye daisies. Perhaps more pleasing to the eye than to the ear, there are scabious and ragwort, hawkweed and toadflax. Rarer is the shy beauty of the clustered bellflower; rarer still, the lovely Loddon Lily growing modestly by a quiet backwater of the Thames in June. On the banks of the river, there are willow herbs, bittersweet, and escaped rapeseed while on the marshy edges of Church Meadow there are spikes of purple-loosestrife – named from an old tradition of tying its stems between teams of oxen to keep the peace.

In July and August, the south-facing slopes of the Clumps stage a kind of Great Exhibition of Thistles – 'Everyone a revengeful burst of resurrection' as Ted Hughes saw them. There are creeping thistles, woolly thistles, musk thistles, greater and common knapweeds, wild teasels and giant burdocks and tall, threatening spear thistles in the damp places of Wittenham

Woods. Also in the woods, in Dyer Lynch's glade, the spring brings spotted orchids and, in the margins, red and white dead nettle, woundworts, comfrey, forget-me-nots and wild garlic.

All of these, and no doubt many more, are to be found when wandering on the Earth Trust lands. Sometimes their beauty reveals itself in a single flower; more often it is the profusion that takes the eye. Common weeds though they be, there is no lovelier sight in all the walks on the Clumps than the dark heads of purple knapweed dancing against the pale gold of the wild parsnips that grow in great swathes in the Iron Age ditch of Fort Hill.

All, of course, have gone as autumn comes to an end, leaving those who walk there looking forward to the first white blossom of blackthorn that foams on the hedgerows in March, bravely leading the world out of winter, though the wind be raw and chill.

❧

Wildflowers have always inspired romantic and lyric poets. But there is a strain in British Romanticism – promoted by Keats, among others – that has long regarded science as in some way the enemy of wonder, poetry and beauty. Scientific knowledge, according to this view, 'makes all charms fly' and 'clips the angel's wings'. Keats even complained that Isaac Newton had 'destroyed the poetry of the rainbow by reducing it to a prism.'

Well, Keats was young and foolish and should have known better. Thankfully, many scientists have taken issue with him, including two of the most distinguished. Physicist Richard Feynman put it tersely in a 1981 BBC interview when he said that studying a flower does not detract from its beauty, 'it only adds.' Stephen Hawking agreed – 'physicists and poets may differ in discipline, but both seek to communicate the beauty of the world around us.'

Though written more than sixty years ago, my favourite example of how scientific knowledge 'only adds' is Loren Eiseley's 1957 essay 'How Flowers Changed the World'. After reading it, I could never see the wildflowers on the Wittenham Clumps in quite the same way again.

Eiseley – an exact contemporary of Rachel Carson, whose 1962 book *Silent Spring* is often credited with launching the modern environmental movement – was both scientist and poet. For many years a Professor of Anthropology and History of Science at the University of Pennsylvania, he was socially awkward, even reclusive, describing himself as 'a fox at the wood's edge'. Others saw him as a modern Thoreau and hailed the poetic writing style so unusual among scientists of the day. As *The New York Times* said on Eiseley's death in 1977, he was 'a scholar and writer of imagination and grace'.

Before coming across Eiseley, I had imagined the world of the dinosaurs to be a world of lush vegetation, tall grasses, huge ferns and exotic flowers. Giant trees and lurid vegetation, maybe. Mosses and ferns, yes. But grasses and flowers, no. The very first flowers did not appear until after the dinosaur age, sixty-five million years ago.

Because the plants of that time relied on wind for sending and receiving pollen, they had no need of anything as showy as petals or colour or scent to attract the attention of insects and birds. Like their ancient descendants the pinecones, their seeds mostly lay where they fell, struggling to grow without either protection or food supply. So poor was the survival rate that millions of their spores had to be released for even one or two to grow to maturity.

Into this dull and wasteful scene, enter the first real flowers to show how things should be done.

The seeds of those flowers were something new. Each one was an embryo neatly packed inside a protective casing along with its own store of food designed to get the youngster started. And instead of just lying where they happened to fall, they had their own transport systems – feather-down to enable them to ride the winds, or hooks and burrs to snag a lift on the fur of passing animals, or a coating of juicy fruit to tempt the birds and animals whose digestive systems would distribute them far and wide.

It was no competition. The new-style seeds, finding their way into every nook and cranny of soil and climate and equipped with their little nutritional starter-packs, began growing up everywhere, putting many of the older plants out of business. The need now was to compete for the attentions of pollinating insects and food-seeking birds and animals, and this meant that the flowers had to get themselves a new wardrobe and start applying the lipstick and the perfume. The world was taking on a different look. And it is exaggerating only a little to say that, from our point of view, beauty was being born.

All this was just a beginning. The price of pollination and passage was paid in the nectar that attracted the insects or in the soft fruits that covered the seed packs – from the smallest berries to the plumpest tomatoes. On top of this, there was the concentrated nutrition packed inside the seed cases themselves, which were virtually pre-packed ready meals. The result of such a dramatic increase in food supply was a population explosion among the insects, birds and animals that gorged on the nectars, fruits and seeds while unwittingly pollinating the flowering plants and dispersing their seeds ever further afield.

Soon the miraculous, riotous processes of specialisation and evolution were in full cry. As Eiseley wrote:

The flowers bloomed and bloomed in ever larger and more spectacular varieties. Some were pale unearthly night flowers intended to lure moths in the evening twilight, some among the orchids even took the shape of female spiders in order to attract wandering males, some flamed redly in the light of noon or twinkled modestly in the meadow grasses. Intricate mechanisms splashed pollen on the breasts of hummingbirds, or stamped it on the bellies of black, grumbling bees droning assiduously from blossom to blossom. Honey ran, insects multiplied, and even the descendant of that toothed and ancient lizard-bird had become strangely altered. Equipped with prodding beaks instead of biting teeth they pecked the seeds and gobbled the insects that were really converted nectar.

Of all these varieties, perhaps the most important of the flowers was the least showy – the inconspicuous but nutrition-packed grasses which soon covered the bare earth. Eventually, they would become today's twelve thousand different varieties, including the timothy grass, velvet grass, foxtail and cocksfoot, that cover the slopes of the Wittenham Clumps.

As these grasses spread across the plains, so herds of new herbivores emerged to feed on them – the mammoths, bison and horses whose non-stop grazing concentrated the fats and proteins of the grass seeds so that soon the herbivores themselves were providing food for new kinds of carnivores: wolves, lions and sabre-toothed tigers.

Eventually, a small band of apes ventured out on to the grass-lands to share in the bounty, occasionally standing upright to peer around for predators or locate new sources of seeds, nuts and fruits. Slow and feeble of muscle, with a delicate constitution and a sensitive stomach, the apes seemed ill-equipped to cope in this fierce, fleet-hooved, tooth-and-claw world. Their only advantage was a larger brain. And eventually it would prove decisive. To supplement whatever food they could gather, they developed tools, group-hunting strategies, and discovered fire for tenderising all that concentrated grass-energy in the flesh of the great herbivores.

Somewhere along the way, an individual in one of these tribes of tool-using apes looked more thoughtfully at the grasses growing on a patch of ground where last year's seed had been thrown or spilt. The rest, literally, is history. As Eiseley put it: 'In that moment, the golden towers of man, his swarming millions, his turning wheels, the vast learning of his packed libraries, would glimmer dimly there in the ancestor of wheat, a few seeds held in a muddy hand.'

Feynman and Hawking are surely right: the beauty of the wildflowers being encouraged to return and flourish on the Wittenham Clumps is only deepened by knowing that they are not just decorative bit players in evolution's drama, but one of its great driving forces. As Eiseley said, 'The weight of a petal has changed the face of the world and made it ours.'

15

SO GREAT A BEAUTY ON THESE ENGLISH FIELDS

The horizon to the south of the Wittenham Clumps seems to follow the gentle contours of a single range of hills, but what we see is two ranges – the southernmost point of the Chilterns and the northern edge of the Berkshire Downs, separated by the invisible valley of the Thames. One of those hills, rising modestly above Cholsey, is Lollingdon Hill, named after Lulla, a Roman farmer who settled in this lonely spot almost two thousand years ago. By a sunken lane at the foot of the hill is an old farmhouse, reachable only by half a kilometre of cart track.

Lollingdon Hill – image by Oxfordshire artist, Anna Dillon

This is Lollingdon Farm, and a more peaceful place it would be difficult to imagine. Yet it was here that some of the greatest literature of war was written.

In the spring of 1914, the farmhouse was rented by John Masefield and his wife, Constance. As he later told the story:

> In the first week of July, 1914, I was in an old house in Berkshire, a house built eight centuries before by the monks as a place of rest and contemplation and beauty. I had never seen England so beautiful as then, and a little company of lovely friends was there. Rupert Brooke was one of them, and we read poems in that old haunt of beauty, and wandered on the Downs. I remember saying that the Austro-Serbian business might cause a European War, in which we might be involved, but the others did not think this likely; they laughed.

❧

Masefield was an anxious, often despairing man. Both his parents died before he was ten and he was sent to live with an unforgiving aunt who felt the boy spent far too much time reading. After three miserable years at boarding school, he was packed off as a cadet on *HMS Conway* to prepare him for a life at sea. He was still only thirteen years old. Four years later, he jumped ship and became a vagrant in New York, living first in Greenwich Village bartending and cleaning hotel rooms before finding a job in a Yonkers carpet factory where he spent much of his pitiful wage on novels and poetry.

Returning to England at the age of twenty-three, he took a job in Wolverhampton, married a teacher twelve years older than himself, and began writing. By the time he and Constance and their two children came to live on the Berkshire Downs, he had already published two novels and a collection of verse. But the great work was still to come. And it began at Lollingdon Hill Farm with the writing of 'August, 1914'.

In form, metre, rhyme, and even in spirit, 'August, 1914' could have been written two hundred years earlier.

Compare this verse, for example:

> *So beautiful it is, I never saw*
> *So great a beauty on these English fields,*
> *Touched by the twilight's coming into awe,*
> *Ripe to the soul and rich with summer's yields.*

with this quatrain from Thomas Gray's famous 'Elegy in a Country Churchyard' written in 1750:

> *Now fades the glimm'ring landscape on the sight,*
> *And all the air a solemn stillness holds,*
> *Save where the beetle wheels his droning flight,*
> *And drowsy tinklings lull the distant folds;*

But old fashioned as it may be, even for its own time, 'August, 1914' is a wonderful piece of writing and quickly established itself as one of the best-loved poems in the English language. Although it presages the horrors and hardships of war, its true subject is the longing of the departing troops for the world they were leaving behind – a world that is represented by 'these English fields' of the Lollingdon Downs.

৵৩

Unlike Rupert Brooke, the companion with whom he had read poetry at Lollingdon in that last summer of peace, Masefield did not rejoice in the outbreak of war. Brooke saw it not just as a patriotic duty but as a glorious opportunity:

Now, God be thanked Who has matched us with His hour,
And caught our youth, and wakened us from sleeping.

For Brooke, the war was a chance for the nation's youth to cast off an indulgent, decadent life for a Camelot of nobility and honour. 'Like swimmers into cleanness leaping' was how he described the battalions of young men marching off to the Western Front.

In practice, there wasn't much cleanness in the trenches. 'Filthied over with broken bodies' was how Masefield was later to describe them. But Brooke did not live to experience the disillusionment that was to come. 'The handsomest young man in England,' as W. B. Yeats called him, died of blood poisoning on the way to Gallipoli.

At thirty-six, Masefield was exempted by age from military service but volunteered to work as an orderly in a British field hospital on the Marne. And like Paul Nash, that other artist of the Downs and battlefields, his letters home ache with the pity of war:

I'm very well, and whenever I look at these poor fellows my soul boils. Nothing else in the world matters but to stop this atrocious thing. Blood and intellect and life are simply nothing … You've no idea of it, you can't even guess the stink of it, from the bloody old reeking stretchers to the fragments hopping on crutches and half heads, and a leg gone at the thigh, and young boys blinded and grey headed men with their backs broken. I never knew I loved men so much. They are a fine lot, a noble lot, I love them all.

Some among his literary friends argued that Masefield was wasting his time and talent as a hospital orderly. This was his answer:

One must not say 'O, it is a waste, your doing such work, you ought to write'; it is not waste; the real waste is war and spilt life and poor, beautiful men bled dead for want of a man to hold them. I could not write, thinking of what goes on in those long slow filthy trains, full of mad-eyed whimpering men.

Returning to Lollingdon, he set about trying to raise money for a mobile field hospital closer to the trenches. Some of those he had helped to care for had taken two or three days to reach the hospital from the Front, often after a jolting journey on rough tracks that added to the pain and panic of their wounds. In the poem 'Red Cross', not published until the eve of another world war, Masefield recalls a surgeon he had met on the Marne:

He said: 'We have buried heaps since the push began.
From now to the Peace we'll bury a thousand more.
It's silly to cry, but I could have saved that man
Had they only carried him in an hour before'.

Frustrated in his plans by French bureaucracy, and moved by the death of his friend Rupert Brooke, Masefield used the £3,000 he had raised to help fund a motorboat ambulance for the war in the Eastern Mediterranean, visiting Gallipoli in August 1915 to see for himself the dreadful human cost of the Dardanelles landings.

֍

Soon afterwards, the War Office commissioned him to tour America to boost support for Britain's cause. Worried by the apparent success of German propaganda efforts, especially in Chicago, he recommended that Britain also enter the war of words. The Germans had made much of the Allied failure at Gallipoli, he reported, and this had struck a chord with Americans who 'neither understand nor pity failure, worshipping success, as they do.' As a result, he was asked to write an article setting out the British view of the Dardanelles Expedition.

It was on his return that the peaceful farmhouse at Lollingdon made its second contribution to the literature of war: over the late spring and early summer of 1916, the article grew into a book that was a homage to the courage of the 'common soldier'. Within a year, *Gallipoli* had sold over forty thousand copies. To this day, it is read and recognised as one of the finest books about war ever written. The attempted capture of Constantinople had failed, with over a quarter of a million casualties among the troops drawn from Great Britain and Ireland, Australia, New Zealand, India, Newfoundland and France (and even more on the Turkish side). But Masefield burned with anger at those who regarded this failure with contempt and no understanding of the courage it had demanded. And like Wilfred Owen and Siegfried Sassoon, he was determined to communicate something of the horror and the heroism to those who felt free to scorn while knowing nothing of what had been endured:

> ... imagine the hills entrenched, the landing mined, the beaches tangled with barbed wire, ranged by howitzers and swept by machine guns, and themselves three thousand miles from home, going out before dawn, with rifle packs, and water bottles, to pass the mines under shellfire, cut through the wire under machine gun fire, clamber up the hills under fire of all arms, by the glare of shell-bursts, in the withering and crashing tumult of modern war, and then to dig themselves in a waterless and burning hill while a more numerous enemy charge them with a bayonet. And let them imagine themselves enduring this night after night, day after day, without rest or solace, nor respite from the peril of death, seeing their friends killed, and their position imperilled, getting their food, their munitions, even their drink, from the jaws of death, and their breath

from the taint of death, and their brief sleep upon the dust of death. Let them imagine themselves driven mad by heat and toil and thirst by day, shaken by frost at midnight, weakened by disease and broken by pestilence, yet arising on the word with a shout and going forward to die in exultation in a cause foredoomed and almost hopeless. Only then will they begin, even dimly, to understand what our seizing and holding of the landings meant.

જાજ

In the following year, 1917, General Haig, commander of the Allied forces on the Western Front, asked Masefield to 'chronicle' the Somme. The battle was over. But his descriptions of what he saw in that now silent, desolate landscape are as evocative of the horror as any live reporting could have been. Inside one crater, for example, he writes that the earth 'trickles and oozes like sores discharging pus, and this liquid gathers in holes near the bottom,

and is greenish and foul and has the look of dead eyes staring upwards.' And it was again at Lollingdon that he began to turn these observations into another wartime classic – *The Old Front Line.*

Through the winter of 1916, Masefield had wandered the fields and farms of the Somme, a landscape that had once been peaceful chalk downs like those of Berkshire but was now 'like a moor in hell … a place of ruin and death, broken

'The real waste is war' – John Masefield
(*photograph: E. O. Hoppé, 1915*)

and blasted out of any likeness to any work of man'. And what strikes him most about the aftermath is the silence and desolation. 'There are few more lonely places,' he writes, 'than the scenes of old battles.' Walking through what had been farms and hamlets, he expects 'at every turn to meet a survivor, but there is none; the village is dead; the grass is growing in the street; the bells are silent; the beasts are gone from the byre and the ghosts from the church.' Travelling what remains of the roads, he imagines the men who 'slept and ate and sweated and dug and died along with them' and foresees that one day 'tourists will walk with ease where brave men ran and dodged and cursed their luck when the Battle of the Somme was raging'.

In a remarkable letter sent home to Lollingdon, he invites Constance to picture the Somme as somewhere she knows well – the area that encompasses both Lollingdon Hill and the Wittenham Clumps – as if the great battle had just been fought there:

> Imagine any 13 miles by 9 miles known to you, say from Goring to Abingdon, raking in Dorchester, Wallingford, Nettlebed and the Chilterns above Goring, you will get a hint of its extent. Then imagine in all that expanse no single tree left intact … Then imagine that in all that expanse no single house is left … Then imagine that in all that expanse there is no patch of ground ten feet square that has not got its shell hole. To say that the ground is 'ploughed up' with shells is to talk like a child. It is gouged and blasted and bedevilled with the pox of war, and at every step you are on the wreck of war, and up at the top of the ridge there is nothing but a waste of big grassless holes ten feet deep and ten feet broad, with defilement and corpses and hands and feet and old burnt uniforms and tattered leather all flung about and dug in and dug out again, like nothing else on God's earth.

In 1917, as the tide of the war began to turn, the Masefields left Lollingdon for Boars Hill, Oxford. Constance had begun to find the isolation just too lonely, and the charms of the ancient farmhouse wore thin when damp and a leaking roof began to affect their son Lewis's health. But before leaving Berkshire, Masefield was finally able to take advantage of its peace to compose the poems published later that year under the title *Lollingdon Downs*.

The Petrarchan and Shakespearian sonnets and other short poems in the collection are still traditional in form. But there is nothing now of the pastoral or bucolic. They are the poems of a shaken world, poems of existential questioning of what human life and consciousness meant at a time when old certainties were fading and new scientific knowledge seemed to be reducing that life to mere cellular activity on the one hand and, on the other, to a disturbing insignificance in a cosmos known to be vaster than previous ages had ever imagined. Unlike 'August, 1914', lines like these could not have been written in any earlier century:

> *What am I, Life? A thing of watery salt*
> *Held in cohesion by unresting cells,*
> *Which work they know not why, which never halt,*
> *Myself unwitting where their master dwells?*

> From 'Lollingdon Downs'

By now well-known on both sides of the Atlantic, Masefield toured America again in 1918, receiving honorary Doctorates from both Yale and Harvard. Invited to read from his work while at Yale, he chose the poem he had composed at Lollingdon on the eve of the Great War that was now ending. And it is perhaps a measure of how much 'August, 1914' still meant to him that he had to apologise to his audience for not being able to continue, stopped by his tears. Later that year, he was able to write to an American friend: 'It is over now … and may this great, kind, generous and truly noble people find its reward in beauty and happiness after all these years of death and hell.'

The last thirty-five years of Masefield's life were spent in a village just on the other side of the Wittenham Clumps. His home there, Burcote Brook, was destroyed by fire shortly after his death at the age of 90. For all of those years, he was the much-celebrated Poet Laureate. But, on sending his poems to The Times, it is said that he still included a stamped addressed return envelope in case they were not accepted.

16

THE WIND BENEATH ITS WINGS

Any collection of essays on the world of the Wittenham Clumps must include the story of the red kite. When I first lived in this part of Oxfordshire more than four decades ago, this magnificent bird of prey was on the very edge of extinction: only two breeding pairs survived in the whole of the British Isles, their nesting sites a closely guarded secret. Not only rare in these islands, it was also on the world's endangered species list. Yet today it is impossible to walk on the Clumps without seeing at least one kite circling for prey, lazily twisting and turning like a wind-blown rag in the sky. And though its range now extends over the Chilterns and beyond, there is no better place from which to see it than from Round or Fort Hill where, instead of being silhouetted against the sky, it can often be viewed from above with its striking wing-markings and shallow-forked, chestnut-red tail feathers catching the afternoon sun.

Yet something about the red kite's return made me hesitate to write about this conservation success story. And as I watch a pair of reds swoop and soar over Church Meadow, disdainful of the

Little victories and big defeats – the red kite returns to the skies over the Wittenham Clumps
(*photograph: creative commons*)

pestering crows, I know that what bothers me is the human story
behind the red kite's fall and rise.

≈≪≫

Back in mediaeval times, the red kite was an everyday sight in
our towns and cities, so valuable as a cleaner-up of streets
stinking with offal and dead vermin that it came under the
protection of a royal decree. In Tudor times, when the streets
became a little less foul, the kite became a nuisance rather than
an asset. Declared vermin under the Preservation of Grain laws,
parish wardens paid a bounty of a penny for every kite beak.
When the birds were also accused, wrongly, of killing game
chicks, they were massacred by gamekeepers using the new
breech-loading shotguns. Now becoming scarce, its eggs were
prized by collectors who began raiding its nests. By the time the
Wittenham Clumps were planted in the 1740s, the red kite was
a rarity. A century later, it had gone altogether from Oxfordshire
and Berkshire. By the middle of the twentieth century, pesticides
had impaired its ability to breed anywhere in England, making
the eggs even more of a collectors' item. And so, by the 1960s,
we were down to those two remaining pairs in a remote valley
in Wales.

Enter Roger Lovegrove, RSPB Conservation Officer for
Wales. Taking up his appointment in 1971, this experienced
ornithologist had never before seen a red kite. When he finally
set eyes on one, high up in Carmarthenshire's Towy Valley, he
was awestruck. 'I thought it just incredible,' he was to say later,
'how something so rare could be as beautiful as that.'
Persuading the RSPB to intensify its efforts, Lovegrove organised a defence of the remaining nesting sites, even persuading
the Army that mounting a round-the-clock surveillance opera-
tion to warn off egg collectors would be good training for the
Gurkhas and the SAS.

From that point on, the fortunes of the red kite in Britain start their long upward swoop. The Welsh kite population secured, conservation groups and the RSPB began importing kites from Spain, Sweden and Germany. In 1989, the first birds were released in selected habitats, including the Chilterns. By 1992, the first imported pair had bred successfully. Today, uncounted thousands of kites roam the skies over Oxfordshire, Berkshire, the East Midlands, Yorkshire, the North East and parts of Scotland. Some are even being re-exported to Spain and France. Common again, the kite's eggs are no longer of interest to collectors.

The diet that sustains this reintroduction includes the kite's usual worms, larger insects, mice, and voles – supplemented by roadkill (about one million animals are killed every year on Britain's roads). For motorists in Oxfordshire, a dead squirrel, pheasant, fox, deer or badger usually means that the kites are on their way, if not already down on the road tearing away at the carcass.

A second, unexpected, source of food has been the leftovers put out so that people can enjoy the spectacular flying display as the kites swoop down, fierce-eyed, talons lowered, to snatch the remains of chops or chicken carcasses from lawns or driveways. According to a survey by Reading University, thirteen per cent of households in Chilterns villages regularly feed the kites. In the city of Reading itself, almost five per cent of families are also putting out food – bringing in several hundred commuter kites every day. The same thing is beginning to happen in Leeds, Gateshead, Manchester, Birmingham and Coventry. Even in London, Shakespeare's 'city of kites and crows', the kite is beginning to make a comeback.

So great has been the success of the reintroduction programme – with even a Royal Mail stamp issued to celebrate the kite's return – that some conservationists are beginning to talk about bringing back other species – perhaps beavers, wolves and pelicans.

Meantime, there are murmurs that the red kite is becoming a pest. I had never quite understood the line in Shakespeare's *A Winter's Tale* – 'When the kite builds, look to lesser linen' – until I read the story of a couple in Glen Esk, Scotland, who cooled off one summer's day by skinny-dipping in a pond and emerged to find their underwear gone. Much later, a gamekeeper found their 'lesser linen' lining a kite's nest. More seriously, there have been complaints locally of people being scratched by kites swooping down to take food from picnics and barbecues. In Stokenchurch, in the Chilterns, a three-year-old girl became frightened to go outdoors after being scratched by a kite that took a fancy to an iced cupcake. In the same village, a seventy-year-old woman was hurt by one of the great birds swooping down on her allotment. Only thirty years or so after the red kite was brought back from near extinction, the first voices are being raised to demand a cull.

ৼৢৢ৵

It will be immediately obvious that the common factor in the ups and downs in the red kite's fortunes – offal filled streets, royal protection, re-classification as vermin, payment of beak bounty, grouse shooting and gamekeepers, egg collectors, pesticides, dedicated conservationists, increase in roadkill, putting food out, possible dangers to children, calls for a cull – is *us*. What has determined whether the bird declines or thrives is *our* needs, choices, and attitudes. We are the wind beneath the wings of the red kite's fall and rise.

And so it is difficult not to conclude that the kite soaring below, sunlight again catching that glorious plumage, is more than an emblem of a successful conservation effort; it is also an emblem of what has been called the Anthropocene – the age of *us* – the age when humans shape the environment as well as being shaped by it.

Some have argued that there is nothing wrong with looking at the natural world from our own point of view, or shaping it to our own ends: we don't, after all, expect wolves or parrots to look at the world from any other point of view but their own. But wolves and parrots don't burn fossil fuels, wrap things in plastic, spray fields with pesticides, shop on Amazon, create deserts or fell forests. Like it or not, the sheer scale and reach of our impact on the planet has indeed brought us into the Anthropocene. And given that we have appropriated to ourselves this astonishing power, we no longer have a choice – we have to face up to the challenge of helping to manage and maintain the integrity of an infinitely complex, interdependent system of living things and natural resources that sustains all life on earth including our own. Equally obviously, it is a task that requires a more informed and sophisticated way of relating to our environment than the old way in which the natural world was treated simply as a supplier of goods, a warehouse, a larder, a reservoir, a refuse disposal site, a mine, a timber yard, a power source, and an occasional provider of interludes of peace, quiet and beauty.

Given that we are well and truly into this new age, it doesn't make a lot of sense to care only about individual elements in the environment – landscapes that we happen to find pleasing or animals that we find characterful or cuddly. The world of the Wittenham Clumps would surely be the poorer without the red kite; yet to the extent that its success depends on roadkill and out-of-date chipolatas, rather than on an intact and healthy ecosystem, it is as much an emblem of the old way than the new.

꿎꿎

The real conservation challenge is probably best seen not from here on Round Hill but through a car windscreen. And like Sherlock Holmes's dog that didn't bark, the clue is not what you can see but what you can't. Remember summers when street-lights were haloed with insects? When headlights and windscreens had to be scraped or washed clean of splattered bugs and flies? Almost without our noticing, it seems, these are sights that have all but vanished.

So much so that Danish science teacher Sune Boye Riis wondered at one point if car manufacturers had come up with some kind of a special coating that kept windscreens clear of dead insects. Thinking more about it, he also realised that when he was riding his bike he didn't have the experience that had been a memorable part of his childhood: he wasn't swallowing any bugs. Mounting a net on a tent pole fastened to his car, he began monitoring the insect catch. Cutting a long story short, Riis eventually became part of an international movement of citizens and scientists that over recent years has been documenting 'the insect apocalypse'.

It would be easy to fill these pages with facts and figures from studies documenting the demise of the insect world. But to take just two examples, England has lost over half of its butterflies in a decade; in Germany, one of the few long-term studies of aerial insect populations has shown a seventy-five per cent decline in the last quarter-century. Very few studies have been made so far outside Europe and North America, and it may be that drawing evidence only from intensively farmed countries gives a distorted view of the global picture. But drawing on the seventy studies available from different countries, the journal *Biological Conservation* has published the first global estimates of the rate of insect loss and feels justified in concluding that 'we are witnessing the largest extinction event on Earth since the late Permian and Cretaceous periods'.

Until recently, the disappearance of insects has been a little-noticed part of the 'sixth great extinction'. Unlike the other five, this one isn't being caused by meteor strikes, volcanic eruptions or ice ages, but by humans. Over the last fifty years, it seems that about three-quarters of all the wild creatures that once ate, dispersed seed, pollinated flowers, aerated the earth, fertilised the land, recycled the nutrients and kept in balance other species have disappeared.

Although this rapid decline is most often presented by images of lonely looking polar bears and sad-eyed pandas, it is the loss of the world's insect population that is proceeding much faster and with much more far-reaching impact. 'If insect species losses cannot be halted,' say the authors of the *Biological Conservation* review, 'this will have catastrophic consequences for the planet's ecosystems and for the survival of mankind.'

We are perhaps used to the word insect being almost a synonym for the insignificant. But we had better recalibrate. E. O. Wilson, the Harvard biologist known as 'the father of bio-diversity', has put the case very simply – 'it is the little things,' he says, 'that run the natural world'. Collectively, the trillions of bugs and flying insects outweigh all the fish in the oceans and all the cattle on the land. And it is these twenty-two thousand types of ants, twenty thousand kinds of bees, and four hundred thousand species of beetle, as well as the millions of insect species not yet identified, that power the world's food chain – turning plant life into protein, feeding birds and mammals, decomposing organic matter, keeping soils healthy and polli-nating three-quarters of all food crops and wild plants.

Insect annihilation has also become noticeable in another way – here on the Wittenham Clumps as in much of Europe. In many parts of Britain, those who once rejoiced in the first cuckoo of spring have not heard its call for a quarter of a century. Those who live in 'the country of skylarks', as Robert Louis Stevenson called the Chilterns, no longer hear their scattering song. The five hundred pairs of house martins that used to nest every year under the arches of Clifton Hampden bridge began to disappear in the 1980s and are now no more. In the damp places of Church Meadow there are no lapwings to be seen, and in the hedgerows hardly any whitethroats. It is possible to walk all the way through Wittenham Wood and down to the Thames without seeing or hearing a bird of any kind. The spotted flycatchers, yellow wagtails, wood warblers, cuckoos, hobbies, yellowhammers, corn buntings, meadow pipits, nightingales – all gone.

But to lament the loss of well-loved species is almost to get back to missing the point. It may be natural to feel more strongly about skylarks than dung beetles, but we can no longer afford to be directed by sentiment. It is we who have brought on the decline of the insects by our use of herbicides and pesticides, by claiming all uncultivated land, by sacrificing forests and meadows, weeds and wildflowers, and by our steady promotion of climate change. In other words, the disappearance of the insect world is another sign of the Anthropocene. And to survive in this new age, our decisions and choices will have to be based on knowledge and concern about the planet's life support system as a whole, rather than on our feelings about the appeal of individual species. Rare, exciting and endangered life forms may make better television, but it is the common ones – and, above all, the insects – that maintain the living systems of our planet. Single-species conservation efforts may have their place, but without a greater concern for the ecosystem as a whole, such efforts will be all charismatic castles in the air with no foundations in the earth.

Other adjustments in thinking are also demanded. Instead of being concerned only about the black-or-white question of extinction, we will need to focus more on the grey areas of functional extinction – the progressive decline of a species to the point where it can no longer play its part in supporting the web of life as a whole. And we also need to escape the habit of measuring what is happening only by our own time and our own memories, leading to a generation-by-generation re-benchmarking that makes the mistake of treating a depleted environment as the norm.

In neglecting the insect world, we seem to have fallen into all of these traps at once. Their presence is less glamorous, their absence less noticeable, and the entomologists who study them less well-funded. Monitoring the health of insect populations can be slow, tedious and sometimes inconclusive because large natural fluctuations make long-term studies necessary if trends are to be reliably established. Few institutions, governments or foundations are as yet willing to pay for such studies. The result, according to Professor Robert Dunn of the Department of Applied Ecology at North Carolina State University, is that 'we've ignored really basic questions – it feels like we've dropped the ball in some giant collective way.'

I am thankful for the return of the red kite, and for the efforts of all those who made it possible. And I cannot feel quite the same turn of joy on seeing a beetle crawling at my feet as on seeing a kite soaring above. But being guided by the head as well as the heart means looking down as well as up.

17

THE GIFT THAT KEEPS ON GIVING

From Round or Fort Hill, it is possible to see more than a dozen of the ten thousand or so parishes that make up the Anglican jigsaw of England. Each parish has its own church, and each church is its own time capsule of treasures, monuments, architectural features, curiosities and artworks that, taken together, form a kind of dispersed national museum of England's heritage.

Take, for example, the parish churches immediately north of the Clumps. In Long Wittenham, the parish church of St Mary has a rare twelfth-century lead Christening font embossed with thirty tiny figures of bishops, long hidden from view behind the wooden panelling that saved it from being melted down for musket shot during the English Civil War. In Little Wittenham,

'Special because they have for so long been so much a part of the story of so many' – St Peter's, Little Wittenham *(author photograph)*

the mediaeval tower of the church of St Peter has a unique window in the shape of the ace of spades that is said to mark the gratitude of Edward Dunch MP, who lost Little Wittenham Manor in a card game with King James II and was given it back on condition he gave up gambling. Even the newest of the parish churches in our view – the 1960s church of St Mary and St Berin in Berinsfield – boasts a stained-glass window that tells the story of the local aircrews that flew thousands of photo-graphic-reconnaissance missions in preparation for the D-Day landings in 1944.

Like many of us, I step inside such churches from time to time and, though not a believer, I often experience that sense of a more than physical threshold being crossed; the sudden drop in temperature; the sense of entering the dank, protected silence of the centuries, redolent of sanctity and mildew.

༄

At every visit, too, I am reminded that my notions of the Church of England are almost entirely drawn from the pages of Austen, Trollope, or Thackeray. If a clergyman were to emerge from the vestry, I would almost expect it to be Mr Collins or Archdeacon Grantly. For those nineteenth-century novelists, the Church of England was a store cupboard of characters and plots and, in Trollope's case, an opportunity for sly and gentle moralising. But what seems most extraordinary to modern eyes about the church of those days is that being a clergyman did not seem to be a calling and required neither theological knowl-edge nor personal piety. It was a 'living' – an income and a house for life. And more often than not, the living was in the giving of the local aristocrat or Lord of the Manor.

On consulting more documentary sources,[16] it appears there was nothing fictional about any of this. The right to appoint a parson to a living, known in law as an 'advowson', was something that could be bought and sold and left to one's heirs. Occasionally, it might even be advertised for auction along with details of the annual income and the charms of the trout stream.

The godfather of this ungodly arrangement was Henry VIII. Having declared himself head of the Church of England and expropriated the lands, properties and rights of the Church of Rome, he began selling his new assets to help pay for his wars. To the purchasers, it seemed only natural that they had also bought the right to appoint the parson. Some no doubt saw it as a Christian duty. Many more saw it as a God-given answer to the problem of how to provide for younger sons, impecunious sons-in-law, or the children of loyal retainers. In particular, it became one of the main ways in which younger sons – who did not stand to inherit the family home and fortune – could maintain the way of life of a gentleman. The essence of being a gentleman – even more than speech or dress, manner or bearing – was not having to earn one's income. However wealthy one might be, deriving one's living from business or trade was a stain on status that might take generations to fade.

The first choice for younger sons was often the purchase of a Commission (three of Jane Austen's brothers were officers, two in the Royal Navy and one in the Militia). As an officer in the Hampshires or the South Devonshires, one received an 'honorarium' – definitely not a salary. Medicine and the law were possibilities, though both came uncomfortably close to working for a living. For those lacking the appetite for any of these alternatives, a church living was a godsend. A clergyman might dine at any gentleman's table, collect his tithe of all that the parish produced, hire a curate for a pittance, and buy a book of sermons to see him through his Sunday obligations. It is all beautifully summed up in one brief exchange in Anthony Trollope's *Framley Parsonage*: 'It does not seem very hard work,' says Lucy Robarts to the parson's wife, who thinks for a moment, before replying, 'But it is very dignified.' Equally revealing is the conversation in

Trollope's *The Way We Live Now*, in which Lady Pomona is shocked to learn that her daughter, Georgiana, is to be seen in the company of a young curate. 'He's got nothing but his curacy!' she exclaims. To which her other daughter replies '… Perhaps papa could get him a living.' Thinking that her brother might also be able to help, she adds 'Dolly has a living of his own that came to him with his property.' But Lady Pomona is not reassured, replying: 'Dolly would be sure to sell the presentation.'

Looking down now at the village of Little Wittenham and its parish church, almost hidden by the ancient yew and chestnut trees on either side of its entrance, it is hard to believe that the power to appoint the vicar was an item of property to be bought and sold. Yet for over three hundred and fifty years that is exactly what it was. After the Dissolution, Henry VIII held the right to appoint the parson of this little church. In 1544, he granted the advowson of Little Wittenham to his Chancellor, Lord Wriothesley, who sold it to Sir Edmund Peckham, who sold it to William Dunch, who sold it to William Hallet, who sold it to Edward Hilliard, who bequeathed it to his son John, who left it to his son William, who sold it to Frederick Bondenham, until, at the beginning of the twentieth century, it was bought by a Mrs M. F. Howland of Doddington Vicarage, Northumberland, after which the trail goes cold.

This was not an unusual history. About half of all the church livings in England at the time were in the giving of private individuals. The rest were owned by the Crown, the Archbishops and Bishops, and the colleges of Oxford and Cambridge. The right to appoint the vicar and collect the tithe in Long Wittenham, for example, was owned by Exeter College, Oxford. To the south of the Clumps, the living of Aston Tirrold was owned by Magdalen.[17] Another Oxford college, Keble, held the advowsons of sixty-nine parishes across England.

Trollope, whose family and forbears included many clergymen, worried that all this would bring the Church of

England into disrepute. In particular, he fretted about 'pluralism' – the practice by which members of the clergy could hold several livings simultaneously, collecting incomes from all of them while employing curates to do the actual work. It was to illustrate this scandal that Trollope gave us the figure of Dr Vesey Stanhope, the clergyman of *Framley Parsonage*, who 'could not attend to his canonical duties in the Cathedral as he was very busy on the shores of the Lake of Como, adding to that unique collection of butterflies for which he is so famous'. Meanwhile, curates were employed on stipends that might be only one-tenth of the income being drawn by the vicar from one parish. Although an ordained clergyman, the curate had no patron or relative to present him with a living yet still needed to keep up the appearance of a gentleman. And it was to represent the curates' plight that Trollope also gave us the figure of the exploited and humiliated Mr Quiverfull and his fourteen children.[18]

❧❧

Did all this really matter? After all, the system had been hardly less corrupt when the church had been responsible for appointing its own clergy. Nepotism, bribery, royal favour, and lay interference had been common, and even in Trollope's times the livings that were still in the giving of Bishops were often disposed of in the same comfortably corrupt manner as those owned by the laity.

But for reformers like Trollope, much was at stake. The church at the time was a force in shaping the character, beliefs and life of the nation. A majority of the population were churchgoers. And the clergy were charged not just with officiating at weddings and funerals but with inculcating a code of morality that included acceptance of one's lot in life, respect for one's betters, good citizenship, and loyalty to the established order and the Crown.

Such responsibilities were discharged both from the pulpit and through the Church of England's control of most of the nation's schools and the offices of local government. Parliament in London was concerned mainly with trade and taxes, the law and the military, and foreign and colonial affairs. Local government was still largely a matter for the parish vestry made up of the parson, the churchwardens, and a handful of prominent citizens and landowners. Until elected local authorities took over at the end of the nineteenth century, it was the parish vestry that levied the poor-rate, chose the Overseers of the Poor, organised what help was available for the infirm and the elderly, allocated the alms houses and attempted to enforce the moral standards of the community by bringing offenders before the ecclesiastical courts. And at a time when illiteracy was common, and the press in its infancy, it was often the nearest pulpit that was relied upon for information and received opinion.

So yes, control over the appointment of the clergy mattered. And the fact that it resided with the landowning classes meant that, by and large, the church could be relied upon to sanction the established order. When it came to the great disputes over Enclosure Acts in the eighteenth and nineteenth centuries, for example, the Church of England tended to stand not with the poor, whose rights to the commons were being removed, but with the landowners, including the church and its clergy, whose yields and profits were rising.

In theory, it is true, the owner of an advowson only had the right to 'present' a candidate to the Bishop, who alone could ordain a Church of England clergyman. But, in practice, refusal was rare – a case of 'this is just a suggestion but let's not forget who's making it'. Nor were the Bishops especially noted for either piety or solidarity with the poor. As Trollope lamented, the ways of becoming a Bishop included being 'a charmer of the royal ear' or 'marrying a bishop's daughter or editing a Greek play, and becoming a tutor to a noble pupil, while quickly adopting the political bias of the pupil's father'.

There were of course honourable exceptions; not all nineteenth-century clergy were like Austen's Mr Collins or Trollope's Dr Stanhope. Even the few parishes to be seen just below the Wittenham Clumps provide several outstanding examples of a more conscientious clergy. The Revd James Clutterbuck of Long Wittenham is still remembered for his half-century of service to the village, from 1830 to 1885, during which time he gave the land to start the Church of England National School, instigated the building of the village hall, and set up the Long Wittenham Friendly Society to encourage saving for pensions. Meanwhile, his wife seems to have been something of a one-woman Ofsted, visiting the village school almost every day to examine the pupils' spelling and the girls' needlework, and make sure they were sitting up straight and imbibing their Bibles. Similarly, the Revd William Butler is still honoured in Wantage, ten miles to the west of the Clumps, for his 'care of three thousand souls.' That care included administering charities, founding civic buildings, campaigning for gas-lighting in the streets, and working to improve the town's water supply, drainage, and sanitation. When he came to Wantage in 1846, there were only thirty-eight children in school; when he retired in 1881, more than seven hundred children were being educated at schools he helped set up.

❧

In Austen or Trollope's time, the village parson had several sources from which to draw his 'living'. There were the fees for performing christenings, weddings and funerals. There was the glebe – church lands which could be worked by employing village labour or leased to local farmers (the living of Long

Wittenham, for example, came with an eleven-acre farm). But, above all, there were tithes.

Tithes were a strange business. Dating back to biblical times, the basic idea was that a tenth of the natural increase of flocks, herds, fields and woods must be handed over to the church. In England, the system went back at least as far as the Saxon King Ethelwulf who formally granted the church the right to collect the tithe. Nearly a thousand years later, in Jane Austen's day, assessing and collecting the tithe was still part of many a clergyman's concerns. *Pride and Prejudice*, for example, gives us the excruciating Mr Collins who impertinently offers Mr Darcy the opinion that the first duty of the clergyman is 'making such an agreement for tythes as may be beneficial to himself and not offensive to his patron'.[19]

Collecting the tithe brought an income, but it also brought problems. Just as there are differences in the tax base of local authorities today – with business rates and council taxes yielding considerably more in south Oxfordshire than in, say, Blackpool or Knowsley – so the tithe collected by the parson varied according to the size and wealth of the parish. But whereas grants from central government go a long way towards evening up the spending power of different local authorities today, no such arrangement existed to redress the imbalance between the tithes collected in Georgian and Victorian parishes. Jane Austen's own father, a clergyman with a small parish and a modest living, could not get by on the tithe. To make ends meet, he took in paying pupils and, on occasion, sold vegetables from a stall by the side of the road. And, as always, Austen's familiarity with these details surfaces in her writing. When Colonel Brandon offers the *oh* living of Delaford to Edward Ferrars in *Mansfield* Park, he is *dear!* careful to specify the 'extent of the parish, condition of the land, and rate of the tythes'.

A more serious problem, for the country parson, was that to collect his full tithe he had to know the source and amount of each farmer's income. And that meant going out into fields, barns and farmyards to record harvests, count cattle, sheep, pigs and hens, and inquire about the output of milk, cheese and honey. For the more sensitive among the clergy, this was an annual embarrassment. And it is to one of Jane Austen's favourite poets, William Cowper, that we owe a glimpse into the tensions, quarrels, and emotions involved. In 1818, the year after Austen's death, he wrote 'The Yearly Distress', a poem subtitled 'Tithing-Time – verses addressed to a country clergyman, complaining of the disagreeableness of the day annually appointed for receiving the dues at the parsonage':

> *The priest he merry is and blithe*
> *Three quarters of the year,*
> *But oh! it cuts him like a scythe*
> *When tithing time draws near.*
> *He then is full of frights and fears,*
> *As one at point to die,*
> *And long before the day appears*
> *He heaves up many a sigh.*
> *For then the farmers come, jog, jog,*
> *Along the miry road,*
> *Each heart as heavy as a log,*
> *To make their payments good.*
> *In sooth the sorrow of such days*
> *Is not to be expressed,*
> *When he that takes and he that pays*
> *Are both alike distressed.*

Cowper, however, seems more sympathetic to the vicar's plight than to the farmers':

> *for well he knows*
> *Each bumpkin of the clan,*

> *Instead of paying what he owes,*
> *Will cheat him if he can.*

The obligation to make small talk with those come to pay the tithe is also seen as a burden:

> *'And how does miss and madam do,*
> *The little boy and all?'*
> *'All tight and well. And how do you,*
> *Good Mr What-d'ye-call?'*

Even more distressing to the good parson, as Cowper saw it, was the necessity of dining with his rustics and having to watch while 'one wipes his nose upon his sleeve' and 'one spits upon the floor'.

But the deeper embarrassment of tithing time was that, once a year, it laid bare the economic innards of the relationship between the clergyman and his parishioners. After a year of aloof pretence of being a gentleman not really in need of an income, the parson now had to soil his hands with the vulgar business of collecting his income from the lower orders, bringing both sides face to face with the reality that it was on the farmer and his family's labour that the vicar's living depended.

With sly humour, Cowper points up this class dimension of the problem: 'Oh, why were farmers made so coarse, / Or clergy made so fine?'

Worst of all, tithing was a time when a mere farmer might even have the temerity to criticize his superior:

> *Quoth one, 'A rarer man than you*
> *'In pulpit none shall hear;*
> *'But yet, methinks, to tell you true,*
> *'You sell it plaguey dear.'*

Several surviving diaries from the period mention that the tensions of tithing time might be eased by food and drink. Parson James Woodforde of Norfolk, for example, records in his diary for 1799 that he held 'a frolic' for all his tithe-paying parishioners, serving roast beef, boiled mutton, plum puddings, punch and beer – 'as much as they pleased'. In a later entry he wrote: 'We had this Year a very agreeable meeting here … no grumbling whatever … We were all very merry and very harmonious.' More tersely, Parson William Holland of Somerset wrote: 'The rest of the Farmers came and paid very well and were cheerful … They made each of them a good dinner and drank strong beer and Brandy and Gin till they were brim-full and then they left me.'

'Frolicking' might go some way towards easing the process, but the rural clergyman still had to make an awkward decision: he could either accept whatever tithe payment his parishioners chose to offer, or he could make his own assessment of each farm's yield and demand that the full tithe be paid. The parson who chose the easy option ran the risk of lowering his income, devaluing the living for future incumbents and offending his patron. If he chose the hard way, he maintained his income and the value of the benefice but risked damaging his relationship with his parishioners and possibly emptying his pews. If he tried to make up for any past backsliding by 'improving' the tithe, the difficulty became all the greater. Again, it was a dilemma that Jane Austen was familiar with. When her own father was planning his retirement, she wrote to her sister: 'My father is doing all in his power to increase his Income by raising his Tythes.' When worrying about her clergyman cousin, Edward, she wrote: 'The living is valued at one hundred and forty pounds a year, but perhaps it may be improvable.' And of course all these concerns surfaced in the novels. 'The late incumbent did not make more than two hundred per annum,' says Colonel Brandon, speaking of the living of Delaford, but is 'certainly capable of improvement.' And pity the poor farmers of Delaford had Lucy Steele succeeded in becoming Edward's wife: her chief concern seems to have been that 'his tythes should be raised to the utmost'.

❧

From up here on the Wittenham Clumps, looking down on the surrounding villages and the spires or towers of their parish churches, it is easy to imagine a Mr Collins doffing his cap to Lady Catherine de Bourgh, or a Reverend Quiverfull eking out a meagre living. But, of course, all has changed. In the second half of the nineteenth century, the winds of reform that opened the Civil Service to competitive examinations and ruffled patterns of patronage in the foreign and colonial service also began to blow away the system of livings and tithes that had long troubled thoughtful supporters of the Church of England.

But not without a struggle. Many argued that patronage and pluralism were essential to keep the church in the hands of the 'right sort' of people. If schoolteachers, clerks, shopkeepers, and even artisans were allowed to apply for ordination, they protested, then the church would soon cease to be an acceptable calling for gentlemen. Even moves to end the scandal of impoverished and exploited curates were opposed on the grounds that raising the stipend would attract the wrong sort of people. But it was to no avail. Patronage was an idea whose time had gone.

In our own times, an even more profound change has come to these parishes – a change made visible on the noticeboards of almost all the churches around the Clumps. St Peter's down there in Little Wittenham, for example, no longer has its own vicar. Instead, it shares a Team Vicar with the similarly emptied parish churches of Long Wittenham, Culham and Clifton Hampden. Nine other parishes on the northern side of the Clumps also share Team Vicars, both of whom, in 2020, happen to be women.

It's the same story across the land. Sundays now see fewer than one per cent of England's population shuffling into the pews of the Church of England, and there are many parish churches where the average Sunday congregation has dwindled to ten or fewer. Nor is the parish vestry any longer the centre of village life. Most of its administrative functions, and of course its schools, have been taken over by local authorities; most of its social and charitable work by the welfare state; most of its preaching by mass and social media.

In all but name, 'livings' are also gone. Patronages remain in theory; the Oxford colleges that own advowsons are still represented on the parish committees that appoint today's clergy. But anyone who wishes to become a Church of England vicar today has to submit to 'discernment', involving examinations and interviews before a Bishops' Advisory Panel. Only if a candidate is judged to have a genuine calling, and to be intellectually and personally suitable for the job, is he or she presented to the Bishop who still has the final say on whether or not to recommend training. Two or three years at theological college, followed by four years' service as a parish curate, leads on to ordination, at which point the ordained vicar is entitled to apply for a parish. Once installed, instead of collecting tithes, he or she will receive a stipend of £17,000 a year, plus free accommodation. For more experienced clergy in large parishes, this stipend may rise to £28,000. That it is a stipend, rather than a salary, is a faint echo of former times when a salary was considered demeaning to a gentleman. But it also has echoes of St Paul, who earned his living as a tentmaker until a gift allowed him to devote all his time to the ministry – this was the precedent cited by the Church of England in 1943 when it decided on the stipend as 'an allowance to allow the priest to live without undue financial worry, [in] neither poverty nor riches.'

Sweeping changes. But perhaps the change that would have surprised Austen or Trollope most is the change in the Church of England's political complexion. In 2014, a trainee Anglican vicar complained in *The Spectator* that he was afraid to confess to being a Conservative. 'At my college,' he wrote, 'there are approximately sixty ordinands in full-time residential training. Of those sixty, there are no more than three or four who would describe themselves as Conservative and the overwhelming majority would call themselves (proudly) socialist. There is also a sizable minority of Marxists.' With its Bishops still entitled to twenty-six seats in the House of Lords, and its pews still mainly blue, there may be some way to go before the Church of England could be described as the politburo at prayer, but there is no doubt that conservative governments of recent years have come under more constant criticism and questioning from Canterbury and the clergy than in any previous century.

◈

Anthony Trollope worried that patronage and pluralism threatened the long-term future of the Church of England. But it was not corruption that would eventually undermine the established religion. It was something more fundamental – and less susceptible to reform.

In 1851, that other great Victorian literary figure, Matthew Arnold, stood on the beach at Dover, looking out across the Channel, listening to:

> ... *the grating roar*
> *Of pebbles which the waves suck back, and fling,*
> *At their return, up the high strand,*
> *Begin, and cease, and then again begin,*
> *With tremulous cadence slow, and bring*
> *The eternal note of sadness in.*

The sadness, for Arnold, was that in the sound of the waves roiling back across the pebbles he heard the 'melancholy, long, withdrawing roar' of the sea of faith.

Perhaps not even he could have foreseen how far that tide would ebb. A century after 'Dover Beach' was written, probably more than half of England's population would still have described themselves as Church of England, though fewer and fewer were regular churchgoers. Thereafter, the decline has been ever steeper: by 1980 the proportion had fallen to about forty per cent, by 2000 to thirty per cent, and by 2020 to just over ten per cent.

Meanwhile, there are sixteen thousand parish churches to maintain, and twelve thousand of them are listed buildings. The cost of their upkeep must, for the most part, be met by their dwindling congregations. On average, the half-million or so churchgoing members of the Church of England donate six to seven hundred pounds a year. But their average age is over sixty. Among young people today, the proportion who identify as Church of England is less than two per cent.

In other words, the future of our rural parish churches does not add up.

Full disclosure: I am not religious and have never attended a Church of England service. The non-conformist church I grew up in, was christened in and married in, closed its doors half a lifetime ago, becoming first a carpet warehouse, then a Bangladeshi community centre. Today it stands empty – its spire dismantled, its blackened brick tower the symbol of blunted belief. The Church of England, as we saw it then, was for the better-off in the city's leafy suburbs. Even so, I cannot help feeling that the loss of our parish churches would be an irreparable tear in the national tapestry. As a well-known American admirer of England's heritage, Bill Bryson, has argued: 'It is impossible to overstate the importance of churches to this country. Nothing else in the built environment has the emotional and spiritual resonance, the architectural distinction, the ancient, reassuring solidity of a parish church.'

Of course, it will be argued that public funds cannot be used to subsidise one particular branch of one particular religion. But it could also be said that our parish churches, or many of them, are a special case. Special in their history. Special in their age and architecture. Special in their monuments, altarpieces, rood screens, choir stalls and glorious stained-glass windows. And special because they have for so long been so much a part of the story of so many. When they were built, almost everyone belonged to the Church of England – or, before the Reformation, the Church of Rome. There were no exceptions and no exemptions from contributions or tithes. The church, with all its faults and hierarchies and corruptions, was of, by and for all the members of the community. It was our forbears' hands that built these churches, their labour that repaired them, their tithes that paid for them, their skills that beautified them.

In other words, our parish churches could be said to be public property that has since been privatised. And this adds weight to the argument that, if they are to be preserved with public money, then they should be returned to the public, loosening their ties to the Church of England and serving the community as a whole. Summing up this argument with some relish, *The Guardian* newspaper in 2017 ran the headline 'England's churches can survive, but the religion will have to go'. In the article that followed, Simon Jenkins argued that our parish churches could recover a central place in community life but that this will not happen if they 'retain their aura of religious exclusivity.'[20]

Others have made the same case, arguing that parish churches are large, empty buildings in central locations and so could be put to use as museums and art galleries, multi-faith centres and retreats, concert halls and festival venues, sports clubs and fitness centres, food banks and farmers' markets, IT help-centres and e-shopping collection points. Some churches have already made moves in this direction – at the time of writing, about thirty parish churches are apparently serving as sub-post offices.

Where the church owns a separate building then of course this makes sense. But the churches themselves? Even as a non-believer, I can't help but think there is something not quite right with this common-sense answer. Maybe, as Simon Jenkins urges, our parish churches do need to lose their 'aura of religious exclusivity.' But if that means no aura at all, then surely they will have lost much of what makes them worth preserving in the first place?

That aura is easier to sense than it is to define. Some would call it spiritual. But I distrust that word when used in a secular sense. Take away a belief in the supernatural, and I'm not sure what it means. But still there remains something about stepping inside a church like the one here at Little Wittenham that is ... special. It is perhaps the feeling of stepping out of the world, or at least into a different kind of space, a sanctuary from the mundane, an atmosphere in which one is invited, sanctioned, to think thoughts other than everyday thoughts about things other than everyday things. For me, at least, it is not the 'aura of religious exclusivity' that appeals: it is the aura of seriousness and time, an atmosphere not of the supernatural but of memory and history, an awareness of the solemn moments in the lives of so many of those who have gone before us – those who have sung and shared, wondered and prayed here across the centuries; those who have hoped and feared, celebrated and grieved; those who have sought forgiveness or consolation; those whose minds have wandered here; those who have looked into themselves and resolved to be better; those who have felt both fellowship with others and the extraordinary aloneness of the individual.

18

AN AFFAIR TO FORGET

She was described by the poet Stephen Spender as one of the most beautiful women of her generation and by the art historian Kenneth Clark as the most beautiful human being he had ever seen. And with the looks went talent, making her a best-selling novelist at the age of twenty-six.

He, too, was 'wonderful to look at – elegant, craggy and irresistibly attractive' – according to the novelist Elizabeth Jane Howard. And he, too, was a literary luminary and a future Poet Laureate.

He remembered their first meeting as a chance encounter in an air-raid shelter during the London Blitz. She recalled losing her heart to him after a brief meeting at a party in 1936. But the encounter that mattered came in May 1941. After reading her *New Statesman* review of his poems, he sent a postcard inviting her to dinner. Following a second date, they spent the night together and 'the tremendous affair' had begun.

To the London literary world, it was a match made in heaven. 'A very fine, good-looking young poet 'married' to a very beautiful and remarkable novelist,' said Laurens van der Post. The problem was that both Rosamond Lehmann and Cecil Day-Lewis were already married. And this inconvenient detail was to gnaw at the heart of one of the most celebrated literary love affairs of the twentieth century.

But what, you may ask, does all this have to do with the world of the Wittenham Clumps? Bear with me.

❧

Little Wittenham Manor – setting for one of the most celebrated literary love affairs of the twentieth century *(photograph: Colin Smith)*

Little Wittenham Manor, settled into its centuries at the foot of Round Hill, could no doubt tell many stories. The original Manor was given by Queen Elizabeth I to the Dunch family, Lords of Little Wittenham for two hundred years. Rebuilt in the late eighteenth century, it was inherited at the opening of the twentieth century by a wealthy young man who rejected a life of ease to face unspeakable hardship with Captain Scott in the Antarctic (Chapter *The response of the spirit*). In 1984, it became the home of Sir Martin and Lady Audrey Wood whose company, Oxford Instruments, built the world's first whole-body MRI scanner and now supplies hi-tech equipment to hospitals across the world. The company also built a fortune for the Woods, who used it to help endow the Earth Trust which eventually acquired the Wittenham Clumps.

It is a remarkable history for one quiet, unpretentious village house. Yet for emotional high drama, and occasional low soap opera, nothing in the life and times of Little Wittenham Manor can compete with the scenes that took place within its walls when the novelist Rosamond Lehmann moved in with her lover, the poet Cecil Day-Lewis, in April 1946.

ويو

Rosamond Lehmann came from a long literary line. Her grandparents counted among their friends Robert Browning, Charles Dickens, George Eliot and Wilkie Collins. Her father, Rudie, founded the Cambridge literary magazine *Granta*. Rosamond herself won a scholarship to read English at Girton College, Cambridge (but could not take her degree because women were not recognised as members of the university until 1948).[21]

While still married to her first husband, but deeply involved in an affair with the man who became her second, she wrote her first novel, *Dusty Answer*. Published in 1927 to no great acclaim, it seemed likely to disappear without trace. To the rescue came the critic Alfred Noyes, a family friend, who wrote a review for the *Sunday Times* which concluded, 'It is not often that one can say with confidence of a first novel by a young writer that it reveals new possibilities for literature … the modern young woman has never been depicted with more honesty, or with a more exquisite art.' There followed a flood of reviews which carried *Dusty Answer* up the best-seller list and into seven reprints in its first twelve months.

It was the 1920s, and many readers, including members of Rosamond's own family, were shocked that a young woman should write so openly about sex. Others rose to acclaim her as the herald of a new generation of liberated women. Rosamond herself was horrified at the fuss and wondered whether she should have followed George Eliot's example and used a male pseudonym. But the controversy boosted sales, as did the enthusiasm of critics like Compton Mackenzie who, after reading *Dusty Answer*, said that he felt 'as if he had been walking about in a magical dawn'.

It was soon after this succès de scandale that Rosamond Lehmann took her first steps in the direction of the Wittenham Clumps. With her new husband, Wogan Phillips, she moved to Ipsden House, just five miles to the south-east. Here, in between having two children and entertaining her literary circle – including W. H. Auden, Stephen Spender, Leonard and Virginia Woolf, Clive and Vanessa Bell, Lytton Strachey, and Guy Burgess – she began work on a new novel. Wogan, meanwhile, painted, drank, typed up his wife's manuscripts and joined the Communist Party (as an artist he was widely perceived to be unbrushed by talent and was disinherited when his father, the first Baron Milford, paid an unexpected visit to the studio at Ipsden and found himself confronted by a full-frontal portrait of a female nude.)

The second novel, *A Note in Music*, was not a success. And neither was the second marriage, which ended when Wogan left to drive an ambulance for the Republicans in the Spanish Civil War. For Rosamond there followed another unsatisfactory affair and another move – this time to the village of Aldworth on the Berkshire Downs just south of the Clumps. And it was while living at Aldworth, frequently spending weekends in London, that she received the invitation to dinner that marked the beginning of the 'tremendous affair'.

❧

Cecil Day-Lewis – along with Spender, Auden and Louis MacNeice – was one of the 'Thirties Poets'. All of them were communists and all except Day-Lewis were homosexual, giving rise to their other soubriquet – 'the homintern'.

After reading Karl Marx, Day-Lewis dithered about whether or not to join the Communist Party and fretted about how best to relate to the proletariat. Soon after graduating from Wadham College, Oxford, he applied for a job with a miners' welfare organisation but was not selected, possibly because he arrived for the interview wearing a dark blue sombrero and a floppy orange bowtie. He then dropped the name 'Cecil' and insisted instead on the initial 'C' (just as Auden had dropped 'Wystan' in favour of W. H.). For a time, also, he omitted the hyphen, but found he did not take to being addressed as 'Mr Lewis'.

While still an undergraduate, he had married Mary King, the daughter of his prep school English teacher. But almost from the beginning, Mary had realised that he would not be satisfied with her. There was already a warning in the lines of the poem he wrote after sleeping with her for the first time: 'No more denied / Seemed no more ideal'.

In search of tranquillity, he persuaded Mary to move to a modest cottage in Musbury, Devon. There he began an affair with the wife of a neighbour, by whom he had a son he refused to acknowledge.

Although eventually a paid-up member of the Communist Party (Cheltenham branch) and a popular anti-fascist speaker, he opted not to join his fellow Thirties Poets who went off to Spain to fight with the International Brigades. Another opportunity to fight fascism came when the call went out for volunteers to join up for World War II. Cecil responded by joining the Musbury Home Guard. When he was eventually called up, he was able to pull enough strings to secure himself a post in the Ministry of Information. And it was while working at the Ministry, writing propaganda pamphlets on the Battle of Britain and Bomber Command, that he invited Rosamond Lehmann to dinner.

Rosamond Lehmann was all that Mary Day-Lewis was not: a literary intellectual, a celebrated beauty, a passionate and liberated woman, and a passport into literary high society from which Day-Lewis felt excluded.

To begin with, the affair was hidden from no one but Mary. Rosamond, in particular, was generous with her rapture, writing to a friend that meeting Cecil was a miracle – 'he was just madly, madly, madly in love with me'. As her biographer, Selina Hastings, has noted, Rosamond had a life-long tendency to believe that men were 'madly, madly in love with me'. But in the case of Cecil Day-Lewis, she was given ample cause. In what would surely have been a contender for the literary bad sex prize, had it existed in the 1940s, he wrote to her: 'darling, darling, darling love, build yourself up next week – plenty of food, rest and exercise – you need all your strength at the weekend – I shall come at you like a tiger, a cloudburst, a toppling mountain, an arrow out of the sun.'

There were just two clouds on this horizon of bliss. The most immediate was that Cecil's position at the Ministry was temporary, leaving him under the ever-present threat of being called-up. The problem was that membership of the Communist Party had saddled him with a file at MI5 (at one time, he had even been followed by secret agents around the unlikely streets of Cheltenham).

The call finally came, despatching him to Catterick Barracks in Yorkshire where he spent all of twenty-four hours in the company of the rank and file, an experience he found less than congenial. Fortunately, one of Rosamond Lehmann's many admirers happened to be Harold Nicholson, Parliamentary Secretary to the Ministry of Information. Just in case, she also wrote to another friend, the novelist E. M. Forster, who also offered to 'pull a string'. By 1941, Day-Lewis was back behind a desk at the Ministry. There he spent the war writing propaganda pieces in the more acceptable company of people like Graham Greene, Osbert Lancaster, John Betjeman and Kenneth Clark.

The other problem was Mary.

Rosamond's husband, wounded in Spain, had already agreed to a divorce. But down in Devon, Mary was patiently awaiting Cecil's occasional visits and believing him to be devoting his weekends to the war effort. When he did make the trip to

Musbury, he wrote to Rosamond in terms which suggest his thoughts might still be in Berkshire – 'the sunshine ... makes me want to take you into the wood over the hill and undress you and kiss the leaf-shadows moving over your body ...'

When the blow finally came, it was cruelly delivered.

Mary opened the post one morning in 1943 to find Cecil's new volume of verse, *World Over All*. It was inscribed 'Mary, with my love, Cecil'. The first poem, like many of those that followed, was written in celebration of Cecil's love for Rosamond Lehmann, to whom the book was dedicated.

Perhaps Rosamond herself was appalled at this way of announcing their affair to Mary. Whatever the reason, it was she who insisted that Cecil go down to Devon and face his wife. The outcome was a compromise, deeply shocking to Mary, by which it was agreed that Cecil would divide his time equally between Aldworth and Musbury. It was a desperate arrangement, and it satisfied nobody. Mary accepted it because it kept alive the hope that her husband would not leave her for good (even going so far as to send parcels of his favourite home-made cakes to Aldworth). Rosamond accepted it because, try as she might, she could not persuade Cecil to make a commitment. Cecil himself acquiesced in the arrangement out of a chronic inability to make a decision.

This characteristic, brilliantly described by Rosamond as his 'aspen hesitation', was Day-Lewis' trademark. Whether it was about hyphenating his surname or joining the Communist Party, he was perpetually in at least two minds about everything. At times he yearned for a busy, glamorous life in literary London; at other times, he craved undemanding rural domesticity. Whether to 'put down roots' or 'continue the journey' was a question forever in balance – and a constant theme in his poetry. And underneath it all there seemed to be a fundamental uncertainty of self. In the poem 'Last Words', he imagines playing the death-bed game of having to sum up one's life in a single sentence and decides that the challenge is not so much what words to choose but '... which of me shall utter them?'

≈≈

Soon after the compromise with Mary was reached, Lehmann's fifth novel, *The Ballad and the Source*, was published to renewed acclaim. Dedicated to Day-Lewis, it was a particular success in America where the *New Yorker* magazine hailed Rosamond as 'the greatest living woman novelist'.

With over half a million copies of *The Ballad and the Source* sold and the film rights bought for $250,000, Rosamond was now financially independent for the first time and immediately began looking for a more elegant home in which to entertain her friends and, she hoped, settle down permanently with Cecil Day-Lewis.

Hopes for the movie ran high. But after Greta Garbo, Ingrid Bergman and Joan Crawford had all turned down the leading role, the backers began to lose interest. A plan to make the film in London also came to nothing when the British Board of Film Censors rejected the script on account of its 'positive portrayal of adultery'.

Meanwhile, Rosamond had found her 'dream house'. And so it was that in the early spring of 1946, Rosamond Lehmann moved into Little Wittenham Manor.

Her ideas on décor were perhaps not quite what Little Wittenham was accustomed to. The walls of the drawing-room, with its views of the Wittenham Clumps, were to be lined in yellow silk, contrasting with curtains and carpets in faded magenta. Over the Adam fireplace hung a Renoir, perhaps lent by Kenneth Clark, while beside a marble table strewn with books and roses was a grey silk divan lit by rose-coloured lamps. Not to be upstaged by her own furnishings, the Manor's new owner often appeared downstairs in silky green and pink pyjamas, her make-up meticulous, her hair sometimes blonde, occasionally violet or pink.

Soon, Cecil Day-Lewis was installed and began using the dining room as his study. Occasionally writing crime novels under the pseudonym Nicholas Blake, he took Little Wittenham Manor as the model for the house featured in *Head of a Traveller* ('a perfect Queen Anne house in the cataleptic trance of white and yellow roses'). Probably he was not aware that the summer-house was said to have been built as a peaceful writing place for Graham Greene, nephew of a previous owner.

To celebrate the move to Little Wittenham, Day-Lewis wrote 'House-warming', a poem in which he imagines a ghost waiting to welcome Rosamond to the Manor. It is a strange poem, not always easy to interpret. The 'ghost by the future made' prepares the house for her arrival, keeping 'its heart aglow' and 'Curtaining, carpeting, lighting all / Your rooms with love ineffaceable'. The last stanzas appear to tell the story of his indecision:

> *Love enmeshed in its own folly –*
> * Mischance or folly –*
> *Expiates a deed for ever undone,*
> *Weeps for all that it could have won,*
> *Of living together wholly.*
>
> *Such is the tenant you'll have beside you,*
> *Often beside you,*
> *Through the spoilt Junes when a gusty rain*
> *Strums fitful arpeggios on the pane,*
> *The dawns when light is denied you.*

Day-Lewis admits in these lines that he is only 'a tenant' at Little Wittenham Manor – and in Rosamond's life. But as she settled into her new home, she stepped up the pressure on him to 'live with her wholly'. Cecil's response was to withdraw, coping with her persistence by switching off his attention and gazing into the distance as if thinking about a new poem.

In desperation, Rosamond eventually sought the advice of her friend and admirer Kenneth Clark, who suggested a simple ultimatum: Mary, or me, but not both. Cecil's response was uncharacteristically decisive. Saying nothing to Rosamond, he took the train down to Musbury and told Mary that he was leaving her and their two boys. To ease the break, and his conscience, he agreed to spend three more months in Devon.

Rosamond, overjoyed, began telling everyone, including her children, that she was going to marry Cecil.

❧

But Mary had not yet given up. By attending to all her husband's needs without reproach, she trusted that, when the time came, he would again hesitate to exchange tranquil domesticity for a life with the more volatile and needy Rosamond.

The three months became four. Then five. From Little Wittenham to Musbury, phone calls and letters implored Cecil's return. Finally realising that her lover could not summon the resolution to make the break, and fearing that she might lose him altogether, Rosamond offered a return to the old compromise. Once again, Cecil began dividing his time between Little Wittenham and Musbury. And, once again, the arrangement satisfied no one.

As the snows gripped Little Wittenham in the winter of 1946-47, Day-Lewis was also frozen into what he called one of his 'black ice' periods of depression. Rosamond described his state of mind as being 'near breakdown' and Mary, too, thought Cecil was 'bordering on insanity'.

With the first thaw, he could bear the strain no longer and decided again to tell Mary that he was going to leave her to 'live wholly' with Rosamond. Again, he took the train to Musbury where he informed his wife of his decision and asked her to drive him back to the station. On the way, she finally broke down. Unable to tolerate her sobbing, he shouted at her to turn the car around. From his study, he picked up the telephone to Rosamond. This time it was Rosamond upon whom the blow fell as she heard him say that, as he had not been able to leave Mary, he had no choice but to end their affair.

This new decision did not, of course, stick. Before long, Cecil was once more dividing himself between Mary in Musbury and Rosamond in Little Wittenham, this time spending two months with each. In practice, he was working for much of the week in London for his publisher, Chatto & Windus, visiting Devon only occasionally and spending most weekends at Little Wittenham.

Again, the arrangement was to prove too precarious to last. Mary still lived in hope, while in the Manor House a fragile bliss alternated with nights of bitter argument.

Now planning a new novel, to be set in Jamaica, Rosamond decided to take a break from the tensions in Little Wittenham in favour of a little light research in Montego Bay. While there, she met Ian Fleming, whom she had known briefly in London (she claimed it was she who first encouraged Fleming to write). Fleming himself was in the middle of an affair with Lady Anne Rothermere at the time, but Lady Anne happened to be away in New York. After a 'heavenly' couple of weeks at Fleming's home, Goldeneye, Rosamond returned to Little Wittenham reassured of her appeal.

Back at the Manor, the old dissatisfactions simmered. Holidays at Bernard Berenson's villa above Florence, and then with Somerset Maugham in Cap Ferrat, provided some relief. But in between times Cecil was back in Musbury with Mary while Rosamond held court in Little Wittenham, complaining endlessly about her situation to anyone who would still listen. After one such evening at the Manor House, Maurice Bowra – now Warden of Wadham College and about to become Vice-

Chancellor of Oxford – threatened to shoot himself rather than be kept up all night listening to Rosamond's complaints. Meanwhile, Day-Lewis's view of the problem seemed to be most clearly expressed not in verse but in one of his Nicholas Blake detective novels featuring a character torn between two women: 'A man so divided, with conscience perpetually working overtime,' he wrote, 'is liable to crack.'

And crack he did. But not quite in the way that either Rosamond or Mary expected.

Soon after Christmas 1949, Rosamond threw a sixteenth birthday party at the Manor House for her daughter, Sally. Among the many guests at Little Wittenham that night were Elizabeth Bowen, Isaiah Berlin, Maurice Bowra, and Peggy Ashcroft with whom Day-Lewis sang a duet. The evening was judged by all to have been a great success. But Rosamond knew something was wrong. Cecil, she said later, had been unaccountably tense. The next morning, he left by train for his office in London from where he wrote to say that he had fallen in love with a twenty-five-year-old actress and was going to live with her. Rosamond threw the letter in the fire. As she later recalled it, Cecil had written that 'every fibre of his being was conscious of the pain he was inflicting' but that there was to be no going back.

అలా

It was after hearing her reading poetry on the BBC that Day-Lewis invited Jill Balcon to dinner in a London restaurant. He was apparently in raptures over her voice, but the appeal was probably not exclusively vocal. Natasha Spender, wife of that other Thirties Poet Stephen Spender, described Jill as 'strikingly beautiful, like a woman you only see on a Greek vase'. After a second dinner together, Cecil walked Jill home past George Eliot's house in Chelsea where they carved their initials into a tree. That night they became lovers.

It may be easily imagined that hell hath no fury like a Rosamond Lehmann scorned. In London herself at the time, she demanded that Cecil face her. He did so, listening to her pleas and recriminations with what she saw as diabolical indifference. The next day, she returned to Little Wittenham, her fury unabated. In letter after letter, and to visitor after visitor, she railed against Day-Lewis as a 'death-cold character'. As for his new love, words almost failed her. But not quite: Jill Balcon was a 'grotesque little piece of human material, this ghastly, over-emotional, fawning creature who unrolled herself like a spaniel at his feet ...'

Day-Lewis, meanwhile, had decided he should probably also mention his decision to Mary and had again taken the train down to Devon. For four days in Musbury, he said nothing. When he did finally get up the courage to tell his wife about Jill Balcon, he found she had already been told – by Rosamond.

Cecil now again asked Mary for a divorce. Mary again refused, and confessed to her private diary: 'I broke down.'

In a couldn't-make-it-up twist, Rosamond and Mary now became allies and arranged to meet in a Mayfair hotel to take tea and discuss how they might rescue Cecil from his middle-aged crisis. Afterwards, Mary wrote that the two of them had got on perfectly well together, though each had wondered which of them would get Cecil back if they succeeded. She also noted, no doubt to her satisfaction, that Mary 'showed no trace of ever having been even pretty'. By the end of tea time, the two women had come up with the idea of persuading Cecil to see a psychiatrist. Cecil agreed – if only to escape from this unexpected pincer movement – and made one visit, under sufferance, to what he called his 'Wimpole Street quack'.

In the months that followed, Rosamond remained in angry denial, certain that Cecil's passion for Jill Balcon had no depth to it. But as the months went by she had to accept that he was not going to tire of this 'chit of a girl'. Finally, she instructed Cecil to come to Little Wittenham to collect his belongings. He arrived at the Manor House with a suitcase and stayed for supper while Jill Balcon waited anxiously in London for his return.

It was to be a long wait. Over dinner, and for hours afterwards, Cecil met all Rosamond's appeals, as he had done so often before, with his poet's stare into the distance. Finally, he picked up his suitcase and asked her to drive him to the station. She refused. He rang for a taxi. None was available. He then set out into the night to walk the five miles from Little Wittenham to the station at Culham. When he eventually reached the main line at Didcot, the last train for London had already left. Taking a taxi the whole way, he arrived in Pimlico at three o'clock in the morning looking, according to Jill Balcon, as if he had been tortured.

Meanwhile, back in Musbury, Mary was also facing up to the fact that the long struggle was over. Reluctantly, she agreed to a divorce. It was 1950, and the law at the time meant that it was she who would have to appear in court to cite her husband's adultery. But citing was not enough. The adultery needed to be proven. Farcically, it was arranged between Mary, Jill and Cecil that a detective should visit the flat in Pimlico and 'discover' Jill and Cecil together. When the doorbell rang, Day-Lewis happened to be out. Jill asked the detective to come back at a later time when he would be more likely to catch them. The divorce became final on September 11th, 1950.

❧

In the end, the question remains: how could two people so privileged by birth and education, so blessed by talent and looks and opportunity, contrive to spend so much of their lives in the emotional and mental anguish that they both spoke and wrote about so often?

In two brilliant books,[22] the critic John Carey has demolished the notion that artists, writers and poets are special souls possessed of greater sensitivity and capacity for empathy with others. In fact, for many of the great and the good of twentieth-century culture it would be easier to make the case for a highly developed lack of empathy. W. B. Yeats, for example, regretted that progress was supplying everyone with the necessities of life, so removing 'the last check upon the multiplicity of the ineducable masses'. T. S. Eliot thought much the same, arguing that newspapers proved the working classes to be 'a complacent, prejudiced, and unthinking mass' and advocating that the numbers receiving higher education should be cut by two thirds. Aldous Huxley held similar views, claiming that education was creating 'an immense class of what I may call the New Stupid'. In Day-Lewis's time, this lack of empathy among writers and poets looking down on the masses from the windows of Belgravia and Bloomsbury seems to have been endemic. From Eliot to Pound, Yeats to Lawrence, Huxley to Woolf, Forster to Shaw, Wallace Stevens to E. E. Cummings, many of those who saw themselves as pillars of high culture often expressed views that were not only crude and bigoted but frequently crossed the line into eugenics and fascism.

This is not to imply that Day-Lewis shared any such views, but only to suggest that artists, writers and poets are not necessarily refined and sensitive spirits whose conduct should be exempted from 'bourgeois morality', or from being summoned to appear before the courts of common human decency. And when stripped of this carapace of moral protectionism, it is clear that Day-Lewis's behaviour towards the women in his life was often heartless and exploitative. There must also be more than a suspicion that he consciously used women as props for his poetry. Rosamond, for example, often feared that he would abandon her and write 'beautiful poetry about separation'. Similarly, Mary commented that Cecil 'makes poetry out of her torture'. Even at the height of the various crises, Day-Lewis himself said that the stress of it all tended to enhance his work by showing me 'poetry everywhere'. On another occasion, he wrote that poets have a tendency to fall in love with a woman in order to 'beget a poem upon her'. This is not the relationship of poet and muse, of Dante to Beatrice, or Keats to Fanny Brawne, or Yeats to Maud Gonne. None of these, surely, would have penned as unpleasant and sinister phrase as 'Beget a poem upon a woman'.

Cecil Day-Lewis and Jill Balcon remained married until the poet's death and had two children together (one of them the actor Daniel Day-Lewis). But, just as with Mary, Cecil began another affair as soon as Jill became pregnant – this time with his wife's close friend, the novelist Elizabeth Jane Howard. She soon ended the relationship, unable to bear the burden of guilt. But not before she too had learnt the lesson – saying that 'Cecil never felt emotion very deeply, but what he liked best, what he needed, was to be unhappily in love but unable to do anything about it. In such situations he wrote some of his best poetry.'

So perhaps the last word on Cecil should be left not to the literary world but to Rosamond's son, Hugo, seventeen at the time, who when told by his mother that she was going to marry Cecil, said 'You're not to! You're not to! He only wants you for his poetry.'

❧

In the case of Rosamond's writing, it seems that her relationship with C. Day-Lewis, on which she expended so much of her emotional energy, was more a distraction than a stimulus.

Like Mary, she suffered much from Cecil's vacillation as he lurched between gushing adoration and utter indifference. But in some measure, also, her suffering had to do with the part of herself in which she took so much pride and satisfaction: her own physical attractiveness.

Discrimination in favour of women who are perceived as being physically more attractive is a prejudice that, even today, goes almost unchallenged. Those judged by others to be physically more attractive generally enjoy advantages in life ranging from choice of partners to chances of promotion. And just as much as whiteness or maleness, physical attractiveness can carry in its baggage a heightened sense of expectation and entitlement.[23] And in the case of Rosamond Lehmann, the effect of this was perhaps carried to an extreme.

That she was highly aware of her own appeal is not in doubt. She delighted in the effect she had on men, taking particular pleasure, for example, in the rumour that T. S. Eliot had told people she was the most beautiful woman he had ever seen. But she seems to have allowed her beauty to become too large a part of who she was, of how she saw herself, and of how she conducted her life.

Such a self-image needed regular fixes of male adoration. Whether it was the octogenarian Bernard Berenson or the teenage friends of her son, she expected, even demanded, flirtation as the price of her favour. And it was this expectation that made her abandonment by C. Day-Lewis so intolerably undermining for decades afterwards.

Other lovers followed. Ian Fleming spent a weekend at Little Wittenham and again invited Rosamond to stay with him in Montego Bay – a visit which went disastrously wrong when she arrived to find that Fleming's partner, who was supposed to have been away at the time, was very much in residence. To make matters worse, Fleming had not mentioned the invitation. Unsurprisingly, the atmosphere when she arrived was less than relaxed and she had to be rescued by Noel Coward who had a house nearby.

On her return to Little Wittenham, she heard that Cecil, finally divorced, had married Jill Balcon and that he was to be made Poet Laureate. Having been one of the greatest admirers of his work, she now considered the honour undeserved, telling her friends he had no great gift.

There followed an affair with Willy Mostyn-Owen, almost thirty years her junior and a friend of her son, Hugo. The young man eventually left for a long stay in Italy. He was later to tell Rosamond's biographer, Selina Hastings, that Rosamond 'was insatiably vain, like a film star in that way … Am I looking beautiful, darling? Am I looking wonderful? … she wanted total attention … and she wouldn't let go.'

Rosamond was now past fifty and finding it difficult to be alone. What she wanted, she told Bernard Berenson, was 'a hand in mine that, once taken, will never let mine go … I don't want affairs with married men who think of me as a sort of luxury cake shop round the corner to be visited when domestic puddings pall.' There was one proposal of marriage, from a solicitor whom she rejected on the grounds that she could never marry a man who kept his teeth in a glass of water and liked to be in bed by ten o'clock.

Little Wittenham Manor House had also, it seems, become a burden to her. Perhaps Cecil's 'ghost of the future' was now haunting her with memories of rejection. In the Summer of 1951, she decided to sell up. One imagines that the old walls, stripped of their yellow silk, might have exhaled a sigh of relief.

❧

There was one more meeting. Finding themselves in the same room at a literary reception, Rosamond and Cecil avoided each other until a mutual acquaintance decided it would liven things up to tell Cecil that Rosamond was waiting at the top of the stairs and wished to see him. When he duly appeared before her, she slapped him hard and loud across the face. Jill, who did not see the incident, said of her husband that he came down the stairs looking 'ashen' and had to be taken straight home.

Sixteen years later, as Day-Lewis lay dying of cancer, Rosamond wrote him a note, asking if he would like to see her. He replied that he was very glad to have heard from her but was too ill for a visit. If things improved, he added 'it would be nice to see you.' He died, quietly, two months later, in May 1972, at the age of sixty-eight.

In her seventies, still believing herself irresistible, still expecting to be courted, still believing that all the men of her acquaintance were at least a little bit in love with her, Rosamond's dependence on her attractiveness made ageing more difficult. At the same time, Rosamond Lehmann the writer was also fading from the public memory.

It was not until her eightieth year that she enjoyed an unexpected revival when Virago, at the time a small publishing company setting out to put women writers on the map, began re-issuing her novels as Virago Modern Classics. Their success became part of the Virago legend and brought Rosamond a new generation of readers. There followed a CBE and an Honorary Fellowship at her old college, Girton. A book of photographs of her life was also published, for the title page of which she selected a telling quotation from Baudelaire: 'C'est un dur métier que d'être belle femme'.

This late re-kindling of fame also brought a new friendship with another of Virago's authors, Anita Brookner, who dedicated her Booker Prize-winning novel *Hotel du Lac* to Rosamond Lehmann. And it is to Anita Brookner, that sharp and subtle observer of character and neuroses, that the last word will be left.

One always had to refer to her beauty, which was not apparent anymore, of course. And she trailed a glorious past behind her, which didn't deceive me for one minute. She was very insecure and very innocent. And I could see that she'd been abandoned. There were lots of names, lots of friends, she gave the impression of an extremely peopled world and life. And yet the impression I had was of a woman sitting alone, inconsolable.

I am indebted for material in this essay to two excellent biographies:
Selina Hastings, *Rosamond Lehmann*, Chatto & Windus, 2002
Peter Stanford, *C Day-Lewis – a Life*, Continuum, 2007.

19

THE SERMON ON THE CLUMPS

Just occasionally, instead of walking around the outside edge of the Wittenham Clumps, I unlatch one of the metal gates and walk through the gloomy glades of beech trees that surmount Round and Fort Hills. There are warnings about not entering in high winds, as some of the trees have been rendered unsafe by fungal decay and, here and there, the damage is visible. Of the half dozen or so older trees, some also bear the scars of carved initials, hearts or dates distorted by the slow, inexorable stretching of the ageing bark.

For some reason, being in the dim light of a beech hanger always seems to suggest metaphors of time passing, of youth's vigour and the wrack of age, of the patient hope of renewal, the old decaying to nourish the new. Perhaps this is because tree metaphors are so ingrained in our way of thinking – the tree of life, the tree of the knowledge of good and evil, the family tree, and even the 'folder-tree' by which we organise computer files. Few, however, have pushed the 'tree-as-metaphor' idea quite as far as the preacher often described as, 'the best-loved man in England.'

Visiting friends at Chrome Hill in Ireland in 1787, John Wesley, the founder of Methodism, hit upon the somewhat whimsical idea of twining two young beech saplings together into a living metaphor of the Methodist and Anglican Churches growing together in strength and unity. The two trees are still there today, locked in their ecumenical embrace. But over the course of two hundred years or so, they seem to have rebelled against being constrained into somebody else's metaphor and have hit back with a metaphor of their own – brilliantly described by Richard Mabey in his book *The Ash and the Beech*:

> Breakaway branches shot off in contrary directions. Sects formed, turbulent eddies of argumentative wood, outlandish bossy gargoyles. Two centuries on, the Wesley Beeches aren't so much a simple parable, holding hands across the wildwood floor, as a rousing hymn to complexity and inventiveness. The point where the graft was originally made has now become a boiling mass of contorted wood and internal braces. The trunks above look disconnected from those below, two entirely new branchings. Born-again trees. Wesley's sermon has become a kind of creation myth, off on its own unruly business.[24]

Rebelling against a metaphor – John Wesley's intertwined beeches at Chrome Hill, Ireland *(photograph: Alex Cameron, Creative commons)*

༺༻

More recently, the German ecologist Peter Wohlleben has put forward the mother of all tree metaphors. Indeed, the story he has to tell in his book *The Hidden Life of Trees* amounts to a virtual sermon on the human condition.

Wohlleben's message is that a forest is a society in which trees communicate, co-operate, and look after each other – through the scents they cast to the winds, through their root systems, through the fungal networks around the tips of their roots, and just possibly through the sounds they make. Trees, it appears, have language.

That language is put to many uses. Acacia trees on the African savannah, for example, can warn neighbouring trees when their leaves are being nibbled by giraffes: not only do the roots begin pumping out bitter toxins to make their own leaves less palatable, they also instruct the leaves to give off a scent that alerts neighbouring acacia trees to do the same. The giraffes themselves, it appears, have wised up to this stratagem and tend to move on – not to a nearby acacia tree, but to one some distance upwind where the message scent has not yet been delivered.

The observant will have noted the shortage of giraffes on the Wittenham Clumps, but something similar seems to be at work among our local beech and oak trees. If a swarm of insects begin to eat its leaves, a beech tree can identify its attackers by their saliva and produce toxins matched to the specific enemy. And it, too, can send a warning to nearby trees to start the defensive process. Even more remarkably, beech, oak and spruce have been known to emit scents that summon the appropriate predators to come and take care of whatever is troubling them.

Although understanding of such systems is still in its infancy, it seems likely that many plants and shrubs have similar abilities. University of California entomologist Richard Karban has shown, for example, that sagebrush can defend itself in the same way. To simulate an insect attack, Karban sat for hours out in the desert taking tiny 'bites' out of the edges of sagebrush leaves with a pair of scissors. When he returned some months later, after grasshoppers and beetles had ravaged the surrounding sagebrush, he found that the leaves near his simulated insect attack had not been touched. When he repeated the experiment but covered the clipped leaves with a plastic bag, the warning system no longer worked. He then analysed the air in the plastic bag and was able to identify the specific scents or 'volatile organic compounds' (VOCs) by which the sagebrush was sending out its warning.

Altogether, around thirty thousand different VOCs have been identified in this 'vocabulary of scent'. Some of them can even be experienced by humans: the sharp smell of freshly cut grass is the scent of VOCs sent out by green leaves when under attack from a marauding lawnmower. And of course we are all used to the chemical messages of the scent given off by flowers competing to attract pollinating insects.

The obvious problem with communication by scent is that it depends on whether and which way the wind is blowing. But researchers like Suzanne Simard at the University of British Columbia have shown that some trees, oaks for example, also have the power to communicate underground. If attacked, an oak can send warning signals to its neighbours via the fungal networks around its roots. Composed of microscopic 'hyphae' – filaments within the cells of fungi – these fungal networks can cover many square miles of a forest floor in a kind of underground fibre-optic cable network or, as some ecologists have called it, an internet of the tree world or 'wood wide web'.

This ability of trees to communicate is only the beginning of the miracle – and the metaphor – discovered by recent research into the secret life of trees. Even more astonishing is the deeper purpose for which the wood wide web seems to be used. For it seems that fungal networks also serve as a means of mutual protection and resource sharing in a kind of arboreal welfare state.

Beech trees, for example, are among one hundred and fifty tree species that are known to be capable of sharing resources and improving one another's chances of healthy growth and survival. The same fungal network that can distribute information and warnings, it seems, can also distribute moisture, sugars, minerals and other nutrients, so that the resources of a forest are shared more equally.

This process first came to light in an undisturbed beech forest near Aachen, Germany, where researchers discovered that photosynthesis – the process by which trees convert light into energy for growth – was happening at approximately the same rate in all the trees, despite some being in stony areas and some in rich, moist soil. Somehow, through their underground network, the beech trees had found a way of sharing resources to give each tree a better chance to grow to its genetic potential. As Peter Wohlleben puts it: 'helping neighbours in time of need is the rule ... Whoever has an abundance of sugar hands some over; whoever is running short gets help'.

The evolutionary rationale behind this mutual support system seems to be that it is to the advantage of each individual tree to live in a forest where its neighbours are doing well. A flourishing overhead leaf canopy, for example, mitigates the extremes of cold and heat, wind and weather, and its wealth of fallen leaves creates a soil rich in alkaline humus, reducing evaporation and preserving moisture. If one or more trees were to sicken and die, the gap opened up in the canopy would allow winds to wreak more damage and sunlight to dry out the forest floor. Because of this, says Wohlleben, 'Even the sick individuals are supported and nourished until they recover. Next time, perhaps it will be the other way around, and the supporting tree might be the one in need of assistance.'

It is a remarkable finding and an irresistible metaphor. But models and metaphors from the natural world can be too glib, and we should not be entirely carried away by the 'lessons of forest society', failing to see the trees for the wood. For in truth those lessons are as limited as they are obvious. The natural world provides as many examples of ruthless competition as of co-operation.

The most obvious reservation to be made about the metaphor of forest society is that its mutual support and sharing system seem to operate only among trees of the same species. The beneficent beech tree that we have been anthropomorphically admiring for its cooperative nature and spirit of egalitarianism is not seen this way by, for example, the oak. To oak trees and many other plants, the beech is a super-efficient monopoliser of both light and moisture, using its natural advantages to deny opportunities for growth to almost everything else in the forest by literally putting the competition in the shade.

The mutual looking-after-each-other that characterises trees of the same species, it seems, does offer a parallel to the evolution of moral or altruistic behaviours within human tribes. But in the globalised societies that humans have created, we also need to evolve the kinds of morality and co-operation that can operate between tribes as well as within them. As many environmentalists have argued, we have entered the age of the Anthropocene in which the human species has become a shaper of the environment as well as being shaped by it. And having come so far and taken upon ourselves so much, there is now little choice but to also accept the responsibilities that come with our power to change the environment we live in. That includes the responsibility for an ethic that can guide relationships within our own societies, between different cultures and nationalities, and between ourselves and the natural world. Evolution itself has helped us towards our limited in-tribe morality. But its blind forces of adaptation will not take us very far in this new age. We will have to work the intra-tribe morality out for ourselves. And trees are not likely to be of much help.

No matter, I am still grateful for Peter Wohlleben's wonderful descriptions of the forest and its invisible processes. As one reviewer of *The Hidden Life of Trees* has written: 'a walk in the woods will never be the same again'.

Wohlleben himself, meanwhile, continues to see tree metaphors in every neck of the woods. In his youth, when he worked as a commercial forester, he saw gnarled and crooked trees as ugly and valueless; today he sees their beauty and character, commenting in passing – 'My own life hasn't always run in a straight line, either'

IV

THE CHANGES THAT THE LAND BEFELL

A HISTORY OF ENGLAND FROM THE WITTENHAM CLUMPS

Illustration: Sarah Woolfenden

As up the hill with labr'ing steps we tread
Where the twin Clumps their sheltering branches spread
The summit gain'd at ease reclining lay
And all around the wide spread scene survey
Point out each object and instructive tell
The various changes that the land befell

Joseph Tubb, 'The Poem Tree', 1844

20

A HISTORY OF ENGLAND FROM THE WITTENHAM CLUMPS

The Wittenham Clumps look out over hundreds of square miles of England's landscape – and thousands of years of its history. The thought must have been with Joseph Tubb when he stood here on Fort Hill in 1844 planning a poem which would 'Point out each object and instructive tell / The various changes that the land befell.' And it was to share the thought with others who might pass this way that he carried his ladder up here on many a summer evening to carve his poem into the bark of a beech tree (Chapter *Tubb, or not Tubb*).

Tubb's poem picked out places in the view that recalled four stages in Britain's story: the Saxon Wars, the Viking invasions, the coming of the Roman legions, and the Age of Monasticism. But there is more, much more within our view from these two low hills. And remarkably, every chapter and turning point in England's long story is represented by something to be seen from the Wittenham Clumps.

Past uprising

The Clumps may have been occupied as far back as six thousand years ago. But a more certain history comes into view when we look to the north-east from Round Hill, towards the nondescript fields just beyond the quiet town of Dorchester-on-Thames. Five thousand years ago, we would have been looking down on a centre of Stone Age Britain. Across those fields was to be seen a double henge of massive timbers approached by a half-mile long processional route aligned with the mid-winter sunrise. No doubt it was as imposing to those who gathered there as any mediaeval cathedral or twenty-first-century sports stadium. And if we wonder how a Stone Age people found their way from far and wide to this ceremonial place without maps or signposts, then the likely answer is that it was the Wittenham Clumps that guided them here, just as they helped to guide returning Lancaster and Wellington bombers to their bases at Berinsfield and Benson during World War II.

Circling the south-eastern side of Fort Hill, the Bronze Age comes into view in the familiar shape of Brightwell Barrow. This lonely outpost of the Clumps is today little more than an eroded mound of rubble and earth, but it remains prominent because, in the nineteenth century, it too was planted with a clump of beech trees. This was the hill and these the trees that Paul Nash painted in the first of his many studies of the Wittenham Clumps (Chapter *No glimmer of God's hand*).

On the horizon to the south, up on the Berkshire Downs, other Bronze Age bowl barrows can just be made out above the villages of Aston Tirrold and Blewbury. It was in Joseph Tubb's time that they were first identified as ancient burial chambers, but they were probably also places where communities gathered for ceremony and ritual – much as today's parish churches are both burial places for the dead and centres of worship for the living. As for those interred in these barrows, they would have belonged to one of several pre-historic settlements unearthed within view of the Clumps. Just this side of Didcot, for example, Bronze Age villagers once subsisted on their monotonous diets where a Tesco Superstore now sells twenty-eight different kinds of ketchup.

Such pre-historic sites are to be found throughout Britain and many other countries, and it is astonishing to think that many of them would have remained undiscovered were it not for something that happened at the turn of the twentieth century here in the fields below the Clumps.

It was during the long, dry summer of 1893 that Henry J. Hewett, tenant of Northfield Farm, Long Wittenham, noticed something odd stealing over his land. Strange geometric markings – circles, squares and straight lines – had begun appearing in the parched crops. Hewett wondered if they might be caused by plants surviving or withering according to what might be in the soil beneath them: an ancient ditch or drain might mean more water was being retained; a stone wall or path might mean less earth and moisture. Not satisfied with speculation, Hewett commissioned a survey. And the rest is history. A very long history of pre-historic, Bronze Age and Romano-British settlement within the great bend of the Thames below the Clumps.

Hewett's discovery at Long Wittenham went on to transform archaeology. When combined with aerial photography, 'crop marks' began revealing thousands of previously unsuspected ancient sites in Britain and around the world. As Robert Macfarlane writes in his magnificent *Underland* essays, they are 'the land's submerged past rising up in parched visitation'.

To see the Iron Age, crop marks are hardly needed. It is under our feet all the way along the grassy embankment around Fort Hill – my own favourite walk on the Clumps. A thousand years before the Christian Era, a Celtic people dug and hauled thousands of tons of earth to create these steep ditch and bank defenses around the palisaded fort that once stood in the place now occupied by the familiar clump of beech.

Within that beech copse, archaeologists have also revealed a much older ditched enclosure thought to be a Bronze Age burial site. And given that Iron Age and Roman communities also buried their dead here, this means that the hill we are walking around has been a hill of death for more than four thousand years. In most cultures and most ages, people have wanted to be able to know and see their final resting place. As Robert Harrison writes in *The Dominion of the Dead*, 'Uncertainty as to one's posthumous abode would have been unthinkable to the vast majority of people a few generations ago'.

Few if any of the Iron Age labourers who built these earthworks would have lived inside the fort itself. More likely, it was a place of ceremony, a statement of tribal power and prestige. Only in times of attack would the whole community have retreated inside the fort with their animals, gold and grain. The homes of these Celts, for perhaps as long as fifteen hundred years, were down there at the foot of Round Hill on the recently excavated fields that adjoin the headquarters of the Earth Trust. It was from there that they might have peered out from under the eaves of their thatched roundhouses to see a giant human effigy made of wicker and reed being hauled into place on the top of the hill. If so, they would probably also have heard the cries of people and animals as they were burned alive inside the 'wicker man', the flames leaping up into the night sky, a sacrificial blaze to strike fear and obedience into the hearts of all who lived within sight of the Clumps.

Or perhaps not. The Celtic priesthood seems to have been literate, but Druidical beliefs forbade them from committing their story to writing and it was left to others to curate their reputation. Of the Celtic Britons themselves – those who built more than two thousand Iron Age forts like this one here on the Wittenham Clumps – not a single man or woman is known by name before the arrival of the Roman legions. And as we walk the earthworks of Fort Hill and wonder about those who lived here more than two thousand years ago, we are forced to acknowledge that there is more mystery about them than about many an earlier civilisation – the ancient Greeks, say, or the Egyptians or Assyrians. What we do know is that they were not the barbarians of Roman myth, covered in skins and woad; they were farmers who wore woven and dyed wool, traded with continental Europe, kept sheep and cattle, produced surpluses of spelt wheat and barley, and constructed wheeled carts that even the Romans admired. If, as Julius Caesar would have us believe, their hair was spiked with white chalk and their bodies and faces covered with mud, woad and blood, then this was only to make themselves more fearsome in battle. Disinterested Roman and Greek sources record the pride the Celts were known to take in their appearance, noting that the men of Celtic Gaul, for example, were punished if their girth grew beyond a certain limit, and that 'no woman can be seen, be she never so poor, in soiled or ragged clothing'.[25]

At the right time of year, this same track around the south-east of Fort Hill may also offer a living representative of that Iron Age past. In late summer, ditch and bank glow with the pale gold of thousands of wild parsnips that might be the descendants of an Iron Age crop. Although the root is bitter and the flowers can cause a skin rash, the wild parsnip is known to have been cultivated in Iron Age times, probably to be mellowed with wine and honey.

Before the path takes us across to the north side of Fort Hill, a glance to the southern horizon offers yet another, very different vision of our Iron Age past. Up there on the escarpment of the Downs runs the Ridgeway Path, thought to be the oldest long-distance road in Europe. In five thousand years of continuous use, it has seen the passage of Neolithic hunter-gatherers, Bronze Age and Celtic tribes, Roman legions, Saxon and Viking armies, mediaeval traders and drovers, and twenty-first-century hikers.

Completing the circuit of Fort Hill and crossing the grassy saddle to Round Hill, the view now opens up to reveal the whole plain of Oxfordshire. Glistening below is the sky-mirror of the Thames and some of the most intensively 'archaeologised' land in the whole of Britain.

But we are not quite finished with the Iron Age yet. Across the Thames, between the Clumps and the town of Dorchester, we can see the raised embankments known as the Dyke Hills. These earthworks, together with the rivers Thames and Thame, surround one of the very few pre-Roman towns ever found in Britain. The site, with its regular pattern of internal roads, is little explored. But even limited excavation has yielded the greatest concentration of Iron Age coins found anywhere in England. Nothing of the town and only this short section of its defensive earthworks can still be seen today. And even this would have disappeared from view were it not for the efforts of General Fox Pitt-Rivers, founder of Oxford's Pitt-Rivers Museum, who, in the second half of the nineteenth century, campaigned against the levelling and ploughing of the Dyke Hills. This, for example, is from the *Saturday Review* of July 2nd, 1870:

> … the fortress at Dorchester and the fortress on Sinodun (Fort Hill) are among the most speaking monuments of the earliest history of our island, and till lately they were among its most perfect monuments. But it is a grievous truth that while we are writing, the dykes at Dorchester are being levelled.

As a result of the protest, the Dyke Hills we see below us became the very first of England's National Scheduled Monuments. Twenty thousand more have been added since.

Roman and Saxon

At some time in the years after 45 BCE, the Celtic tribes living at the foot of the Clumps would have witnessed the arrival of a new era in our history when the first of the Roman legions appeared in the Thames valley. Perhaps some of those who lived here were recruited, or forced, to work on the Roman road that was to come up through the Goring Gap and the villages of Mackney and Brightwell before climbing what is now the quiet bridleway that skirts the Clumps to Wittenham Wood. At some uncertain point, that road crossed the Thames to arrive at what became an important Roman town. And in our view from the Clumps today, it is Dorchester-on-Thames that best represents the next four hundred years of our story.

Here on the streets and in the marketplace within Romano-British walls that can still in part be traced, those local British tribes would first have encountered novelties that would become a permanent part of British life: literacy and law, tribute and taxes, roads and aqueducts, baths and temples, planned towns and square-built public buildings in stone or brick. Here, too, they would have seen for the first time the beginnings of Britain's commercial life: stock-taking, written accounts, trademarks, advertising, and coins for shopping at street stalls selling things never seen before, such as onions and garlic, peas and turnips, apples and pears. For the well-off there would also be villas, one of which – investigated by Channel 4's *Time Team* in 2004 – stood here on the lower slopes of Round Hill to the north-west of the public car park. Nearby, on the land surrounding the Earth Trust headquarters, a Roman farmstead thrived for three centuries, though of villa and farm only a bronze lampstand, a spear, a few cups and coins, and fragments of pottery and mosaic have been unearthed.

Stopping to sit for a while on the bench at the top of the north-facing slope of Round Hill, we see below the two villages that represent the next chapter in our history – and the one that would see the birth of the nation we know as England.

There had been occasional raids across the North Sea by Germanic tribes during the four centuries when Britain was a northern outpost of the Roman Empire. But after the legions left in 410 CE, the raids became an invasion. Over the next two centuries, Angles, Saxons and Jutes from what is now Germany and the Netherlands took possession of most of present-day England. In the process, they either assimilated the Britannic tribes or drove them to the Celtic fringes of Cornwall, Wales, Scotland and Ireland.

Among the very earliest of these Saxon settlements in England were the two villages we see below us now. Both pre-date Saxon times. Local historian Ian McDougall has suggested that 'Long and Little Wittenham rank among the oldest inhabited communities in the whole of Britain.' But the name by which the Wittenhams are known today is nonetheless a Saxon name. One possibility is that it meant 'Witta's Ham', signifying the *ham* (or village) of Witta, a West-Saxon chieftain mentioned in the *Anglo-Saxon Chronicle*. Another possibility is that the name refers to the meeting place of a *witan*, an Anglo-Saxon council. Either way, the lands below were the heartland of the West Saxon people known as the Gewisse who settled here in the fifth and sixth centuries and occupied dozens of the towns and villages within our view including Abingdon, Radley, Didcot, Blewbury, Culham, Cholsey and Sutton Courtenay.

If from this vantage point our eyes follow the mile-long country lane joining the two Wittenhams, we eventually arrive at a Saxon site that has only recently been brought back from the past. Here, in 2016, at the eastern edge of the village of Long Wittenham, a team from Oxford University's Department of Archaeology uncovered the remains of a seventh-century Saxon complex that may have been the home of Witta. Since then, the thatched, wattle-and-daub feasting hall has been rebuilt by volunteers using materials, tools and techniques that are as close as possible to those available to the Saxons themselves, including a rickety timber crane. The hall is now home to Wulfheodenas, a living history society that seeks to 'recreate the military aristocracy, their warrior retinues and the mead-hall culture of the 6-7th Century Early Anglo-Saxon.'

Turning from the Wittenhams to look down on Day's Lock and the Thames, just below Round Hill, we see the place where England's history took its next decisive turn. The exact spot is not known, but in the year 635 CE an Italian or Frankish monk named Birinus, sent from Rome by Pope Honorius I, baptised the West Saxon King Cynegils in the waters of the Thames near Dorchester.[26] It was to be these Saxons, under King Alfred the Great, who would eventually unite all of England as a Christian nation.

Close to the baptismal place, Cynegils gave Birinus land on which to build the modest wooden church which over the centuries became the great abbey church of Dorchester-on-Thames – in the centre of our view looking north-east from Round Hill. Birinus is said to have founded other churches near the Clumps, at Ipsden and Checkendon, but his name will forever be associated with Dorchester. And when we hear the Abbey's great tenor bell tolling out over the countryside, that too is a reminder of the events of 635 CE: cast into the rim of the bell is the inscription: '*Protege Birine quos convoco tu sine fine.*' (Do thou, Birinus, protect forever those whom I summon).

Turning back to look down once more towards Long Wittenham, perhaps just within sound of that bell, we see a patch of land that is another reminder of the coming of Christianity. At the western end of the village, in the area known as Free Acre, excavation has revealed a Saxon cemetery that spans several centuries and tells its own story of the conversion: the later the burial, the more likely the body to be aligned east-to-west in the Christian tradition.

Wessex and England

For all their peacefulness, it would be an unusual day on the Wittenham Clumps if one were not to hear a Puma or Chinook helicopter clattering into the skies from RAF Benson on the far side of the Thames. And the place from which they are lifting off represents another moment in the making of the nation. Here, at the Battle of Benson in 779 CE, King Offa of Mercia defeated King Cynewulf of Wessex and took control of most of what was to become England, following up his victory by establishing a stronghold and look-out post here on the Clumps.

Offa's peace was not to last. Within a few decades, all of the Saxon kingdoms were under threat from a new wave of invaders from the lands known today as Norway, Sweden and Denmark. A hundred years after their initial landings in the North, the Vikings arrived here in the Thames valley, torching Dorchester in 869. Soon, Wessex was the only Saxon kingdom offering resistance. But what a resistance it was. And it would lead eventually to Alfred the Great and his successors uniting all of England.

The long struggle is represented in our view from the Clumps by the town of Wallingford, just to the east and partly visible from Fort Hill. Established and planned by Alfred himself, Wallingford is Britain's finest surviving example of a Saxon town. To be seen still are the original ninth-century street grid and half of the mile or so of earthworks that, together with the Thames, formed the town's defensive perimeter. Saxon 'herringbone' masonry is still there to be seen in the north wall of St Leonards church.

Less precisely, the struggle that led to the creation of England is also represented by an uncertain hill somewhere on our horizon to the south. All that is known about the Battle of Ashdown is an unhelpful detail from Alfred the Great's biographer, Asser, who tells us that on a cold, damp January morning in the year 871, the Saxon and Viking armies met around 'a thorn tree of stunted growth'. But more than a thousand years of oral history testify that the place was Lowbury Hill near the village of Aston Tirrold. There, the twenty-two-year-old Prince Alfred, after camping overnight at Moulsford, took up a position to await the arrival of his brother, King Ethelred, whose army was camped on Blewburton Hill just within sight of the Clumps. Ethelred, who had picked up pious habits in Rome, thought it might be prudent to start the day by attending Mass at All Saints Church in Aston Upthorpe. Not knowing when his brother might show up, and afraid of losing the advantage of his position, Alfred launched his own forces in a great clash of shield walls up on the Downs. Ethelred eventually put in an appearance and by nightfall the Saxons had won a great victory. 'Five Earls were slain,' says Asser, 'together with many thousand pagans covering with their bodies the whole plain of Ashdune.' The Victorians felt confident enough to identify the exact battle site and even to organise school visits. Thomas Hughes, Berkshire-born author of *Tom Brown's Schooldays,* wrote of one such visit: 'We are treading on heroes. It is sacred ground for Englishmen – more sacred than all but one or two fields where their bones lie whitening. For this is the actual place where Alfred won his great battle, the Battle of Ashdown, and made England a Christian land.'

The Vikings did not see it that way. A century or so later, they again marauded their way down the Thames valley, this time torching Wallingford where their leaders, Swein Forkbeard and Cnut the Great, sensitive souls both, cut off the hands, ears and noses of the hostages they had carried with them from Oxford.

All change

Academic historians don't much like the idea of significant dates, arguing that great changes come about only slowly and subtly. But there are moments of sudden upheaval that change almost everything – power and governance, laws and land ownership, culture and language. The Norman conquest of England in the year 1066 was such a moment. And it is again represented in our view by the town of Wallingford.

It was here that William the Conqueror crossed the Thames[27] after the Battle of Hastings on his way to take London and the throne; here that the Saxon Earl Wigod[28] opened the town gates to welcome the invader; here that the formal submission of the English was made by Stigand, Archbishop of Canterbury, at the head of a delegation of Saxon Bishops and thegns; and here that the Conqueror built the first and one of the finest of the five hundred castles by which the Normans eventually controlled all of England. If the wind is in the right direction, and if we are here on the Clumps towards nine o'clock in the evening, we might even hear a reminder of those far-off days in the sound of the bell tolling out, as it does every evening, from the tower of St Mary's Church to signal the end of the extra hour before curfew that the Conqueror granted to the people of Wallingford in return for assistance received.

Wallingford may have been treated leniently, but what followed elsewhere amounted to perhaps the greatest upheaval ever seen in this land. Almost overnight, the entire governing class of Saxon England was replaced by Norman knights and nobles who had gambled on sailing with the Conqueror. Everywhere, Saxon Manors were seized and redistributed to the victors – the Manor of Didcot, for example, being handed to the Norman knight Henry de Ferrers.

Similarly, England's great churches were now to be ruled by Norman Bishops and rebuilt in the Norman style. At Abingdon Abbey, just north-west of the Clumps, the Abbot was imprisoned and his place taken by a monk from the great Abbey of Jumièges in Normandy. In Dorchester, the Bishop was deposed to make way for a warrior-monk from the Abbey of Fécamp, also in Normandy, who is thought to have been a relation of the Conqueror and may have fought alongside him at Hastings. To complete the rout, the English language was also deposed, replaced by Norman French as the official language of England.

By the time the King's commissioners arrived to make their entries in the Domesday Book for the villages around the Clumps – Long and Little Wittenham, Brightwell and Sotwell, South and North Moreton, Aston Tirrold and Aston Upthorpe, Appleford and Sutton Courtenay, Blewbury and Cholsey, Bensington (Benson) and Lollingdon – the men and women who dwelt there were outsiders in their own country. Even the layout of their land was reorganised as their new overlords imposed the Norman open field system that was to endure until the Enclosure Acts of the eighteenth century. To this day, the view from Round Hill includes the two great fields established by Norman reorganisation: North Field and West Field.

In contrast to the violent upheavals of the Conquest, the eleventh and twelfth centuries in our history were also the Age of Monasticism. Widespread corruption had not yet corroded the monastic ideal, and it was a time when monks and monasteries contributed much not only to religious life but to the preservation of books and learning, to the care of the sick and the poor, to the development of the woollen trade, and to pioneering new methods of land and water management.

Monasteries were not new in England. The period known as the tenth-century monastic revival had been led by Bishop Aethelwold from his abbey at Abingdon, where a school was established centuries before scholars settled in Oxford. Today, the abbey is a ruin, obscured from our view by the low, wooded hills around Culham. By the time of the Conquest, Aethelwold's Abingdon had become the spiritual centre of England, standing at the head of a movement that numbered over fifty monasteries and nunneries up and down the land. Two hundred years later, under the Normans, that number had grown to almost a thousand. Many of those abbeys, monasteries and cathedrals are still today among the glories of England, dominating the skylines of our towns and cities and gracing some of our loveliest rural settings.

This Age of Monasticism is represented by the fine Augustinian abbey of Dorchester-on-Thames. The original wooden church of St Birinus was long gone, replaced by a Saxon stone cathedral. But within a hundred years of the Norman Conquest, this too had been replaced by the abbey we see from the Clumps today. And though the Augustinians in their white habits and black cloaks are no longer to be found in its cloisters, there is one item of furniture from the twelfth century that can still be seen: at the entrance to the nave is the magnificent lead christening font that has been used to baptise the people of Dorchester for over eight hundred years.

Plague and Plantagenet

As the new abbey was being built, the country around it was once more being convulsed by conflict. For twenty years, the lands we see below were crisscrossed by the armies of the Norman Queen Matilda and the Angevin Stephen of Blois as they fought for the throne of England. So brutal was the conflict that the *Anglo-Saxon Chronicle* described it as a time in which, 'The land was ruined and it was openly said that Christ and his saints slept.'

These two bleak decades of civil war also came to an end within our view from the Clumps. In the summer of 1153, the armies of Stephen and Matilda faced each other across the Thames at Wallingford. Matilda occupied Wallingford Castle. Stephen had his stronghold on the opposite bank of the river at Crowmarsh (the site of the present-day housing development known as Stephen's Fields). With no decisive battle in the offing, the church brokered the Treaty of Wallingford. Under its terms, Matilda agreed that Stephen would be King, and Stephen agreed that Matilda's son would succeed him. Stephen obligingly died within the year and the treaty came into effect, giving England Henry II, one of its greatest Kings, and launching the Plantagenet era that lasted for the next three centuries.

One of Henry's first acts was to summon a Great Council at Wallingford, at which he rewarded the town with a Charter of Liberties, allowing its citizens a degree of self-government and the right to hold a regular market, a tradition which continues to the present day. It is this Charter of 1155 that is proclaimed on Wallingford's coat-of-arms to be seen at the entrances to the town.

For over five hundred years, the place where the Treaty of Wallingford was signed was one of the most magnificent castles in all of England. Today, it is a few forlorn outcrops of preserved walls standing in a peaceful Thameside meadow. But having given England the Plantagenets, its role in the nation's history was far from over. As the home of Edward the Black Prince and Bad King John, it also featured in the long struggle with the English barons that led to the signing of the Magna Carta in 1215. Many times during that prolonged conflict, King John retreated to Wallingford, one of only four English towns mentioned in the Magna Carta itself.

At about the same time, about eight miles north of the Clumps and just within our view from the top of Round Hill, a quieter step in Britain's history was being taken. There had long been teachers in the small Saxon town by a ford on the River Thames. But after Henry II banned Englishmen from studying in Paris, students and scholars began to drift instead towards Oxford. All went well for a few years until an incident occurred which saw two of the University's dons hanged by the town authorities, following the suspicious death of a woman. Fearing further town-versus-gown hostilities, a few of the scholars decamped to set up a similar institution in the remote fenlands of East Anglia. Six hundred years were to pass before another university was founded in England.

For most people in Britain, the great events of the following century were not the endless wars and rumours of wars that rolled across Europe, but an enemy that left its black-edged calling card with almost every family. In June of 1348, the Black Death arrived on the south coast, carried by fleas on black rats travelling the Silk Road from Asia. Within twelve months, England's population had been reduced by perhaps a third. Wallingford and Didcot were particularly hard hit, losing half their populations. Two other Oxfordshire villages, Tusmore and Tilgarsley, disappeared altogether from history.

For a poignant reminder of this most mournful period in all of our country's story, we can look to the Parish Church of St Mary in the village of Ewelme, five miles to the east of the Clumps. Faced by an enemy as undiscriminating as the Black Death, it had become common for the wealthy to make donations to religious houses in the hope of buying protection in this world or salvation in the next. At the same time, the preoccupation with death led to a fashion for tombs adorned with two stone effigies – one on top showing the deceased in earthly finery, and one below depicting a ghoulish corpse or skeleton. Most were the tombs of men, but in the east transept of St Mary's is a striking example of a 'cadaver tomb' of a woman – Alice de la Pole, Duchess of Suffolk and granddaughter of the poet Geoffrey Chaucer.

Church coffers, side chapels, altarpieces and statuary may have thrived on desperate donations, but the Black Death was unappeased. Only a dozen years later, the dread swellings in armpit and groin began to appear again, this time claiming one in five of Wallingford's people and leading to the closure and decay of seven of the town's eleven churches. It did not, fortunately, close the Queen's Head pub, just across the Thames, which had first opened its doors seven years earlier in 1341 and which managed to survive both the Black Death and the new bridge at Abingdon that sent Wallingford into a long economic

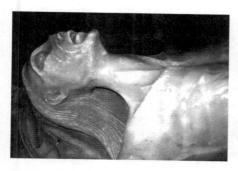

Lower part of the double 'cadaver tomb' of Alice de la Pole, St. Mary's Parish Church, Ewelme *(photograph: Simon Cope, ShareAlike 2.0)*

decline. Let us hope it will also survive the 2020 Covid-19 pandemic, which, at the time of writing, has closed all forty-seven thousand pubs in the United Kingdom.

Golden Age to Civil War

As we have seen, Wallingford Castle gave England the Planta-genet dynasty. And with a little license, it can also claim to have given us the Tudors.

Katherine of Valois, beautiful wife of Henry V and dutiful daughter of the King of France, was given Wallingford Castle when her husband died on campaign in France. Here she settled down to bring up her infant son. She was twenty-one years old and forbidden to marry again until her son reached maturity. But this was the age of courtly love and chivalric flirtation, and it was here at Wallingford that Katherine began an affair with the Keeper of the Royal Household, the Welsh nobleman Owen Tudor. Legend has it that Owen caught Katherine's eye when he fell into her lap while dancing, or, Darcy-like, when he emerged from a dip in the Thames. Either way, it was Katherine and Owen's grandchild who, as Henry VII, brought the Wars of the Roses to an end and founded the Tudor line. No romance at Wallingford, no Henry VIII or Elizabeth I.

The great historic change brought about by the Tudors was the break with Rome, the dissolution of the monasteries, and the transformation of England into a Protestant country. And it is a change once more represented in our view by the abbey just across the Thames – one of almost nine hundred abbeys, monasteries, priories, convents and friaries to be stripped of status and wealth by Henry VIII and his chief minister Thomas Cromwell. Taken together, the expropriated religious establishments had owned about a quarter of the landed wealth of England.

The immediate cause of the dissolution – Henry's matrimonial enthusiasms, his spat with the Pope, his determination to place himself at the head of the Church of England, and his pressing need for funds to fight wars – is among the best-known episodes in English history. But it was preceded, and perhaps made possible, by the unpopularity of the monasteries themselves. Influential figures, like the great European scholar Erasmus, were accusing the Church as a whole of growing lax and wealthy, and of profiting from the gullible and the pious by promoting the veneration of bogus relics – charges from which our local abbey was not exempt. The monks of Dorchester had long made good business out of dubious relics of St Birinus. As for 'moral laxity', the parish was scandalised by at least one incident concerning the monk John Shrewesbury, who was said to have abducted a woman and smuggled her into the tower of the Abbey inside a trunk.

Given an Abbot of sufficiently adaptable convictions, some religious houses were allowed to continue serving as cathedrals, abbeys or parish churches under the new Church of England. In the case of Dorchester, the saviour of the abbey was a local merchant, Sir Richard Bewfforeste, who offered the King one hundred and forty pounds (perhaps £100,000 in today's money) on condition that the roof would not be stripped of lead and the abbey itself allowed to continue to serve as a parish church. It may also be that the magnificent christening font, cast in the time of William the Conqueror, was included in the deal as it was one of the few lead fonts to survive the Dissolution. The Abbey's holy of holies – the shrine of Saint Birinus – was not spared and became one of thousands of works of art and statuary to be destroyed. The Abbot of Dorchester, John Mershe, and five of his Canons held on to their posts by 'subscribing to the king's supremacy'.

The nation-changing event of the following century was of course the English Civil War. And within view of the Clumps there are reminders large and small of the great conflict between Parliament and Crown which cost the lives of a greater share of England's population even than World War I. To the north stands Oxford, Civil War headquarters of King Charles. To the south-east lies Wallingford, whose great castle was the last of the Royalist strongholds to fall. But it is the two small villages directly below the Clumps that most intimately illustrate the turmoil of the times.

Long Wittenham leaned towards the King; Little Wittenham towards Parliament. Or at least the Lord of the Manor of Little Wittenham, Edmund Dunch, favoured the Parliamentary cause. Indeed, he may not have had a great deal of choice as his wife, Mary, was the aunt of Oliver Cromwell. She also happened to be the sister-in-law of the great Parliamentary hero John Hampden, who had first defied the King by refusing to pay Ship Money and whose arrest, along with five other MPs, was the spark that ignited the decade-long conflict.

Cromwell, it seems, stopped at Long Wittenham on his way to attend a family wedding at Little Wittenham, and local lore has it that he was sitting under a mulberry tree at the Old Farmhouse while Royalist troops were searching for him at the other end of the village. It is not known whether John Hampden also visited Mary Cromwell, but from the Clumps we can just see, five miles to the north-east, the site of the Battle of Chalgrove Fields where Hampden was fatally wounded by a carelessly loaded pistol that blew up in his hand.

Little Wittenham may have had a family connection with the Civil War, but all of the countryside below the Clumps saw something of the conflict as the armies of both sides, cavalry and foot soldiers, marched across Oxfordshire and Berkshire. Most villages, hoping to minimise losses of crops and livestock, tried to avoid taking sides. But it wasn't an easy game to play. In the village of Blewbury, five miles to the south-west, the Fuller family of Hall Barn (still a fine home today) is said to have wined and dined Royalist and Parliamentary forces within hours of each other. Often there was no choice about which side to support: on a spring morning in 1644, the village of East Hagbourne, now almost contiguous with Didcot, woke up to find itself generously hosting the Earl of Essex and ten thousand Parliamentary troops.

Nor was there a great deal of choice in the matter of religion. As Cromwell's Puritans gained the upper hand, Long Wittenham's churchwardens and Overseers of the Poor were required to ensure that every man over the age of eighteen signed a promise to keep the Protestant faith. Out of a hundred adult men in the village, only fifteen were able to sign their names, the rest putting their mark. Fortunately, the churchwardens were less compliant in the matter of the parish christening font, which was quickly encased in wood to prevent it being melted down for musket shot. Another two hundred years were to pass before the cladding was removed and the original Norman font saw the light of day. It stands today in the nave of St Mary's – one of only thirty lead fonts to have survived the Civil War.

What did not survive, unfortunately, was Wallingford Castle. By the spring of 1646, all of the other Royalist strong-holds in the Thames valley – Oxford, Abingdon, Reading – had fallen to Cromwell's forces. Wallingford was besieged but held out under its commander, Colonel Thomas Blagge, who refused to surrender unless the King himself ordered him to do so. Conditions inside the castle were reported to be grim, the troops unpaid and underfed. Forty hogsheads of stinking beef had to be burned or thrown into the Thames. In July, the King finally gave the order to surrender and Blagge paraded his thousand foot soldiers out of the castle with full honours. After marching the agreed ten miles from Wallingford, the men disbanded and drifted away to their homes.

Despite being able to withstand a three-month siege, the Wallingford Castle of the Civil War was not the stronghold it had once been. Much of its timber and lead had long ago been shipped down the Thames to enlarge Henry VIII's residence at Windsor. But the strength of its fortifications and its dominance of the Thames crossing was such that Cromwell fretted about it falling once more into enemy hands. In November 1652, his Council of State ordered its demolition. Today, all that remains of one of England's finest castles, often besieged but never taken, is the central mound of the motte and the steep banks on which the great walls once stood.[29] Perhaps some small consolation is to be found in the slim spire of St Peter's Church, rising just across the road from what was once the castle's main entrance. The original St Peter's was destroyed at the same time as the castle itself. A hundred years later, when it was decided to rebuild, the commission was given to Robert Taylor, a frustrated sculptor who named his son Michael Angelo Taylor. Little else of Taylor's work survives, but in his designs for the new St Peter's Church he gave Wallingford what is surely one of England's loveliest spires.

As for the villages surrounding the Clumps, there was at least one benefit from the loss of the castle as they were no longer required to pay garrison taxes. For the townspeople, the only other advantage was a supply of stone from the castle walls, some of which can be seen today in the re-built tower of St

Some of the stones from Wallingford Castle were used to re-build the tower of the parish church. One is inscribed with the name of the Royalist Mayor of Wallingford who was dismissed from office by Oliver Cromwell and re-instated by Charles II *(author photograph)*

Mary-le-More, the parish church just behind Wallingford's town hall. One of those stones, in particular, is a reminder of the divided loyalties and fluctuating fortunes of those times. To be found just above eye-level on the south-west buttress of the tower, it is inscribed: 'Will Loader 1653'. Loader was the Royalist Mayor of Wallingford who was dismissed from office by Oliver Cromwell and re-instated by Charles II.

Meanwhile, Edmund Dunch, Lord of the Manor of Little Wittenham, was suffering the opposite fate. He had been rewarded for supporting Cromwell by being ennobled. Five years later, the monarchy was restored and all titles bestowed by Cromwell rescinded. Baron Burnell of East Wittenham became plain Ted Dunch again.

A final reminder of the religious conflicts of the seventeenth century is the crooked brick and thatch cottage known as French's House at the southern end of Long Wittenham's main street. One of the oldest houses in Oxfordshire, it was the home of 'John French of Longwitam, anno 1530' – as recorded in *Foxe's Book of Martyrs*. Charged that 'he believed not the body of Christ, flesh, blood, and bone to be in the sacrament', he was judged a heretic and 'wrongfully molested' by the church of Rome.

The great divide

Less than a generation after the Restoration of the monarchy, the Clumps again witnessed a turning point in England's history. As Christmas 1688 drew near, Long Wittenham looked on anxiously as lines of foreign infantry and dragoons came through from their camp at East Hendred. It was a far larger invasion than that threatened by the Spanish Armada exactly a hundred years earlier, but the villagers need not have worried: the foreign soldiers marching down the length of the village that day meant not a new conflict to disrupt their lives, but the coming of the 'Glorious Revolution' and the age of William and Mary.

To secure a Protestant succession, five Earls, a Viscount and a Bishop – known to history as the 'Immortal Seven' – had invited William III, Prince of Orange, to invade, promising support if he would come with a small army and install his Protestant wife, Mary, niece of King Charles II, on the throne of England. William's response was to come with a large army and install himself on the throne with Mary as co-regent. So it was that the 'Protestant Wind' brought an army of thirty-five thousand men up the English Channel. And like William the Conqueror, six centuries before, William of Orange chose to advance down the Thames valley on his way to claim London and the crown. Save for a brief skirmish at Reading, there was little resistance. But what the villagers around the Clumps saw arriving that December morning was nonetheless a revolution – setting Britain on its modern course as a Protestant country ruled by Parliament rather than the Divine Right of Kings.

After William and Mary came an eighteenth century that it is possible not only to see but almost to touch from here on the Wittenham Clumps. For we have arrived at the years when these, the oldest surviving hill-top beech clumps in England, were first planted.

Planting clumps of trees on hilltops was part of an eighteenth-century vogue for 'ennobling landscapes' and was often as much about displaying fashionable taste and proclaiming landed wealth as improving the view. But the real business of the day was the Agricultural Revolution, which transformed England's countryside by closing off thousands of acres of common land to create large, enclosed fields more suited to new methods of crop rotation and selective cattle breeding. Parliamentary Enclosure Acts came to almost every village in our view during those years – and are visible today in the miles of apparently harmless hedgerows that divide up the fields we see below.

Two specific places in our view represent this great change brought over the land by the agricultral revolution. From Brightwell Barrow, looking East across the Thames, we see the village of Crowmarsh Gifford where Jethro Tull devised and perfected the horse-drawn drill that sowed seed with economy and precision, instead of being scattered haphazardly by hand as it had been since Biblical times. Tull went on to write *The Horse-hoeing Husbandry: or, An Essay on the Principles of Tillage and Vegetation*, a work that helped revolutionise agricultural methods across Europe (and became a manual for Voltaire at his farm in Ferney).

Tull is the most influential but not the only pioneer of the agricultural revolution to fall within our view. A mile or so to the north-west, just across the River Thame from Dorchester, we see the tiny eighteenth-century hamlet of Overy, whose Manor House bears the stone inscription 'WHD 1712'. This was the home of the gentleman farmer William Davey, who became a pioneer of the new agricultural techniques. So well-known did he become that King George III – 'Farmer George' – is said to have arrived one day on horseback to inspect the farm.

All these are reminders of the great rural upheaval that vastly increased the yield from England's soils in the eighteenth century. But they are also reminders of the great social and economic divide that was widened and consolidated at this time in our history. Out of the Enclosure Acts and the new profits from farming grew the world of the all-powerful landed gentry and the richer clergy, giving us the society of Jane Austen with its class system based on lineage, land, and the absurd but all-powerful notion of 'good blood'. The dark side, much less celebrated in novels and drama, was the impoverishment and suffering of the rural poor, and the even greater horrors of the Atlantic slave trade from which so much of the wealth invested in land and stately homes was derived.[30]

One side of this great divide is represented in our view by Little Wittenham Manor, which in the early eighteenth century was owned by Mr and Mrs William Hallet. Their names are little-known today, but the portrait of the couple – Thomas Gainsborough's *The Morning Walk* in the National Gallery – is instantly recognisable as one of the best-known portrayals of the wealthy and fashionable of Georgian society. It was the Hallets who pulled down the original Manor House of Little Wittenham and began building the present Manor. They also used their wealth to confer at least one benefit on the village – building the footbridge across the Thames by which generations since have been able to walk between Little Wittenham and Dorchester.

The other side of the times, the heartlessness and economic injustice on which this fashionable society flourished, is represented by the village of Nuneham Courtenay, four miles to the north of the Clumps. Or, rather, not seen. In 1761, the Earl of Harcourt had the original village demolished, along with its mediaeval church and village green, in order to remove the lower orders from his view and clear the way for landscaping the grounds of Nuneham House. The incident is widely thought to have been the inspiration for one of the most famous political protest poems ever written. Oliver Goldsmith's 'The Deserted Village' tells the story of Sweet Auburn, a mediaeval village destroyed to clear the way for landscaping a rich man's park. It is a passionate cry against an age in which 'One only master grasps the whole domain' and 'the rich man's joys increase, the poor's decay.' The Sweet Auburn of the story is widely believed to have been Nuneham Courtenay.

England's wooden walls

As the eighteenth century wore on and the beech trees of the Clumps grew to maturity, modern Britain was coming into being around them. Robert Walpole was in Downing Street as Britain's first Prime Minister. Roads and stagecoaches were linking up towns and cities. The British East India Company was laying the foundations of the Raj. Cook's voyages were completing the map of the world. The Quakers were striving to abolish the slave trade. Convicts were starting to be transported to Botany Bay. The first of the Factory Acts – and the first laws outlawing trades unions – were making their way through Parliament. In continental Europe, the French Revolution was shaking the foundations of the old order. And in Little Wittenham, the foundations of a new bridge were being built to replace the unreliable ferry across the Thames.

Meanwhile, the great event that marked the last quarter of the eighteenth century was the loss of the American colonies and the birth of the United States. And this momentous development is also represented by one of the villages here below the Clumps. In Brightwell (today Brightwell-cum-Sotwell) in the year 1712, Margery Bernard, wife of the Rev. Francis Bernard, gave birth to a son, also called Francis, who was orphaned when he was six years old but who rose to become the colonial Governor first of New Jersey and then of Massachusetts. It was Bernard's high-handed approach and contempt for the colonists and their leaders that is widely credited with helping to turn a protest over taxes into a revolutionary war leading to the Declaration of Independence and the creation of the United States of America (Chapter *The man who lost America*).

Francis Bernard was not to know it, but the new nation born of the revolution on the other side of the Atlantic would establish itself with the help of a contemporary who also lived and worked close by the Wittenham Clumps. William Blackstone, Recorder of Wallingford, Oxford's first Professor of Common Law and the greatest jurist of his age, was a poor public speaker and had failed to make a career as a barrister. But what he lacked in fluency on his feet he more than made up when sitting down with his pen. At his desk in Castle Priory on Wallingford's Thames Street, he set about bringing order and coherence to the hotchpotch of custom and precedent that was England's Common Law. The result of his labours was the most famous of all legal textbooks – Blackstone's four-volume *Commentaries on the Laws of England*.

As well as being fundamental to the English legal system, Blackstone's *Commentaries* were also the foundation for building the rule of law in the new country across the Atlantic. Seven years after Blackstone's death in Wallingford, James Madison and the delegates to the Constitutional Convention of 1787 looked to the *Commentaries* for guidance in drawing up Federal law and the American Constitution. To this day, Blackstone is cited by the US Supreme Court when ruling on questions of precedent. Not long after I had first read the blue plaque commemorating William Blackstone at St Peter's Church on Thames Street, where the great jurist is buried, I happened to be visiting the classic New England town of Litchfield, Connecticut. Here, the Tapping Reeve Law School opened its doors in 1784 as the first independent law school in America. In pride of place on the shelves, above the original desks and furnishings, sits a set of leather-bound books written here below the Clumps in Wallingford – Blackstone's *Commentaries on the Laws of England*.[31]

The opening years of the nineteenth century were dominated by the wars with Napoleon's France. Though far from the battlefields, our view from the top of Round Hill takes in at least one reminder of those times. Following the line of equally-spaced lime trees that pick out the narrow road running north-west from Little Wittenham, the eye is led to a wood where the road enters the neighbouring village of Long Wittenham. From here on the hill, it looks like any other small woodland on the Oxfordshire plain. But this is not just another beech copse. Its trees are English oaks, more than ten thousand of them, planted by volunteers to commemorate the two hundredth anniversary of Nelson's victory at Trafalgar. It is one of twenty-seven such woods planned in Britain and Northern Ireland, each one named after a different ship in Nelson's fleet that famous day. The one we can see below is Neptune Wood – named for *HMS Neptune*, the ninety-eight-gun third ship-of-the-line that played a major part in the battle. With her hull holed and her rigging shot to pieces, it was the *Neptune* that towed *HMS Victory* into port at Gibraltar with Nelson's body on board. In 2005, Captain Freemantle, a descendant of the *Neptune's* commander, attended the ceremony marking the opening of the Wood.

The idea came from the Woodland Trust and was intended to commemorate not only the victory at Trafalgar but also the part played by the oak in defending our island over so much of its history. It is said that between three and five thousand mature oaks were needed to construct just one ship-of-the-line. Oak trees, as the diarist John Evelyn described them in the eighteenth century, were 'Britain's wooden walls.'

The notion of thousands of twenty-first-century volunteers planting an oak wood for each of Nelson's ships at Trafalgar might seem to some to be tinged with British eccentricity. But for the real thing, we would need to travel forty miles south-west of the Clumps to Wiltshire, just this side of Stonehenge. Best seen from a hot air balloon, or on Google Earth, the landscape here appears to be dotted with seemingly random clumps of trees. In fact they represent, in precise formation, the British and French ships that fought the Battle of the Nile seven years before Trafalgar. Only nineteen of the original thirty-one clumps remain today, each featuring taller beech trees at the centre to represent the billowing sails with maples and hawthorns around the edges to represent the hull. Now that's eccentric.

Rail and romance

After a succession of poor harvests, the rural poor were facing the winter of 1830 with dread. The agricultural divide of the eighteenth century had grown ever wider as new farm machines had brought widespread underemployment. And as the cold weather closed in, rural anger boiled over into what became known as the Swing Riots.[32]

Starting in Kent, where over a hundred of the new threshing machines were smashed, the riots soon spread to the villages below the Clumps. Crowmarsh and Benson saw the earliest rioting, soon followed by Burcot and Clifton Hampden, where a threshing machine was smashed at Latham's farm. From there the protest spread three miles west to Appleford. When prosecutions were brought, the magistrates and judges sided with the landowners, not least because they usually were landowners. In all, nineteen of the rioters were hanged, six hundred and forty-four imprisoned, and four hundred and eighty-one transported to the penal colonies of Australia.

The miseries of both the rural and urban poor, and the hypocrisy of so many establishment figures, are well-known features of the Victorian Age. But so is its can-do spirit of enterprise. And one example of its astonishing achievements appears every few minutes in our view to the south where, even on moderately sunny days, ribbons of reflected light glimmer from the windows of the trains shuttling between London and the West Country. Since 2017, it has been easier to pick out the line by the ungainly galvanised steel gantries that supply cleaner electric power. But if we had been standing here in the middle of the nineteenth century, we would have seen the same route traced across the land by the slowly dispersing plume of steam from one of the Brunswick green engines of the Great Western Railway.

The Victorian Age had hardly begun when the merchants of Bristol commissioned the twenty-nine-year-old Isambard Brunel to build 'the greatest railway in the world'. And build it he did, surveying every mile of the route on horseback and personally designing the bridges, tunnels and stations right down to the ornate lamp posts on the platforms. Not a man of modest visions, Brunel also designed the *SS Great Britain,* the largest passenger ship in the world and the first iron ship to cross the Atlantic, aiming to make the Great Western Railway the first stage of a route linking London and New York.

If Brunel's original plan had been followed, the great age of railway construction would not have been represented in our view from the Clumps. The direct route would have taken the line south of the Downs, via Newbury and Marlborough. But a combination of landowners' protests and the potential profits from a branch line to Oxford dragged the track to a more northerly trajectory, bringing it under the Clumps on its way to Swindon and the West and provoking cynics to say that the initials GWR stood for the 'Great Way Round'. The branch line to Oxford was supposed to begin at Abingdon, but this was again opposed by landowners, including Oxford colleges. As a result, an earlier branching off point was chosen, so transforming the small Saxon village of Dudcote into the still-expanding commuter town of Didcot that we see below the Clumps today.

When it finally opened in 1844, the Didcot-Oxford branch line was routed close by the Clumps at Culham. And in doing so it also gave our view an example of the stern paternalism and panicky morality of the nineteenth century. The Parliamentary Bill to permit the branch line to be built was initially defeated because Oxford University feared that providing undergraduates with easy access to London might lead to 'improper marriages and other illegitimate connexions'. The Chancellor of the University at the time was the Duke of Wellington, the victor of Waterloo, who objected to all railways on the grounds that they encouraged the lower orders to 'move about'. A railway to Oxford was even more objectionable, in the Iron Duke's eyes, because it threatened the city with 'tourists' and 'loungers'. The Bill was eventually passed, but with the stipulation that undergraduates could only be sold tickets to 'suitable places' and that the University should patrol the new station to prevent young men from visiting dens of iniquity such as Ascot.

Today, the Victorian Age is perhaps most visible in the many Gothic Revival buildings in our cities, towns and villages. With its nostalgic looking back to a pre-industrial age, the style sits oddly with the forward-looking spirit of the Great Western Railway and the Great Exhibition of 1851. Yet it just as surely left its mark in every corner of England, including in one of the villages here under the Clumps.

Clifton Hampden is a picturesque hamlet of timbered and thatched mediaeval quaintness. But in the early eighteenth century, it was a poor, run-down place of a few dishevelled cottages and an almost totally ruined church (the churchwarden had been excommunicated in 1779 for failing to keep the place in good repair). Things began to look up when the Director of the Great Western Railway, George Henry Gibbs, became the new Lord of the Manor. Or rather when his son, Henry Hucks Gibbs, a future Governor of the Bank of England, used the railway magnate's legacy to begin renovating Clifton Hampden in his father's honour.

The man he hired for the job was George Gilbert Scott, leading light of the Victorian Gothic revival and architect of many famous buildings, including the Albert Memorial (his grandson, Giles Gilbert Scott, was also an architect and gave England its familiar red telephone box). Scott and Gibbs began by rebuilding the church that stands on a promontory above the Thames. They went on to restore much of Clifton Hampden, making it into the Victorian-mediaeval hamlet we see today. Over a twenty-year period, Scott tidied up the facades of the brick and thatch cottages, some dating from the sixteenth and seventeenth centuries, and built a Gothic lych gate, a parsonage, a schoolhouse, and the famous brick, six-arched Gothic bridge over the Thames. Whether or not it is true that Scott sketched the design for the bridge on his starched linen shirt-cuff over dinner with his patron, he and his builder, Richard Casey, made a fine job of it. As the artist and Thames punter George Leslie wrote in 1881: 'The bridge is of red brick, with ribbed Tudor arches, which will become very beautiful when age has toned them a little.' As of 2020, it is possible to see exactly what Leslie meant: a few years ago, a section of the brick parapet was demolished by a wayward truck and has been replaced by raw-looking new coping, though it is 'toning' rapidly under the influence of today's traffic.

A thoughtful feature of Scott's bridge was the small triangular bays above each pier, which allowed pedestrians to step inside and enjoy the view of the Thames and the rebuilt church while being safe from coaches and horses. Inevitably, children have long seen these small pedestrian havens as fine places from which to drop various items into the river. In the unenlightened seventies, they were even encouraged to do so by a teacher at Clifton Hampden Junior School, who suggested the class write messages to be placed inside a glass coffee jar and dropped from the bridge. Twenty-eight locks and weirs later, the jar floated out from the Thames Estuary into the Channel. After another year had passed, a reply came back from the children of the Drevivier family of Tours who had found the jar on the beach while on holiday in Brittany. When the children of Long Wittenham wrote to inform the Thames Water Authority, they received the official reply – 'Highly remarkable and slightly reprehensible.'

Stop Line Red

As we enter the twentieth century, all the villages around the Clumps have their memorials to those who gave their lives in the Great War. But in our view to the south, there is another particularly poignant reminder. Where the Berkshire Downs descend to the Thames, sits Lollingdon farmhouse. Here, the future Poet Laureate, John Masefield, wrote the long, nostalgic poem 'August, 1914'. And here, too, he turned his field notes into the wartime classics *Gallipoli* and *The Old Front line.* After his visits to the battlefields of the Somme, it was to these Downs that he returned, more appreciative than ever of their peace and beauty, and here, too, that he wrote the book of poems entitled *Lollingdon Downs.*

The years between the two world wars were marked by economic depression. But for many of those in work, this was also the beginning of what has been called the Age of Leisure. And that beginning would have been visible from the Clumps in the passing to and fro of steam trains like the 'Cornish Riviera Express'. For not only were the lower orders beginning to 'move about', they were having the temerity to take holidays by the seaside. And for thousands of working families in the inter-war years, it was the chocolate and cream livery of the GWR's carriages that came to symbolise that annual week or two on the beaches of Devon and Cornwall, places that until then had been remote and unvisited.

It was not to last. Soon troops replaced tourists on the trains as Didcot became an army camp and a supply depot. Now the

view from the Clumps took in some of the historic moments of
World War II as the Luftwaffe struck at RAF Harwell and the
Wellingtons and Lancasters took off from Berinsfield to join
the bombing raids on Hamburg, Dresden, Bremen, Cologne,
Essen, and Berlin. Meanwhile, the slopes of Round Hill were
ploughed up to plant wheat and barley in the dark days of 1941
when Britain faced the threat of starvation. To add a little meat
to the menu, a supply of rabbits from the burrows of
Wittenham Clumps were sent every week to London butchers.

By 1944, photo-reconnaissance had become the key to
ending the war and it was at this time that the Clumps saw
hundreds of missions flown by British and American planes
from Mount Farm airfield, Berinsfield, and RAF Benson, just
across the Thames.

Later that year, the Clumps also witnessed the beginning of
the end. On the site where Didcot power station would one day
be built, the spring and summer of 1944 saw the shuttling in of
supplies for the D-Day landings. And on the evening of June
5th, an observer looking west from Round or Fort Hill would
have seen a flotilla of Horsa gliders being towed into the skies
from RAF Harwell, heading for Normandy. Onboard were the
one hundred and eighty men of the Ox and Bucks Light
Infantry and the sixth Airborne Division under the command
of Major John Howard. A few hours later, just after midnight on
June 6th, 1944, the flotilla drifted silently down towards the
bridge over the Orne and the Caen Canal. Landing just metres
from their target, the Green Jackets took and held the bridge,
preventing the German command from bringing up reinforce-
ments to oppose the Allied landings. The bridge was later
renamed Pegasus Bridge after the insignia worn by the Green
Jackets that night. Major Howard himself eventually retired
here to Burcot and is buried at Clifton Hampden.

As for the end itself, that too was marked on the Clumps by
a bonfire that lit up the night sky, along with all the other fires

lit along the hills and Downs, to celebrate VE night – just as they had been to celebrate victory in the time of the Spanish Armada and the Napoleonic Wars.

All these are reminders of the Second World War. But also within our view are a few almost-forgotten mementos of that conflict. Those who walk the Thames towpath will, every so often, come across an incongruous concrete bunker overgrown with weeds. These Type 22 and 28A pillboxes with their mediaeval-looking gun slits are the remains of 'Stop Line Red' – the chain of reinforced bunkers and fortified houses by which it was planned, or hoped, to halt the expected German invasion in the months following the evacuation of Dunkirk. And it is a measure of the desperate heroism of those days that one and a half million Home Guard volunteers were prepared to man twenty-eight thousand of these bunkers at 'stop lines' running east-to-west across the country in an attempt to defend rivers against an army that would have already crossed the Channel. On the peaceful Thames Path, these brutal bunkers are reminders of Britain's 'darkest hour'. Less conspicuously, other reminders can occasionally be found beside our country lanes as we glance into a ditch and see a few broken concrete blocks almost hidden by vegetation. As the years go by, fewer and fewer will recognise them as 'dragon's teeth' – the anti-tank cubes that were also part of 'Stop Line Red'.

Power to the future

The most recent chapters in Britain's history are of course visible in every direction from the Clumps today: in the heavy-yielding agricultural lands that are almost devoid of insects, birds and wildlife; in the 1960s 'new village' of Berinsfield built by the Council just across the Thames; in the distant BMW factory that turns out almost a thousand Minis a day; in the once-humble cottages of farm labourers that are now million-pound weekend homes; in the sprawl of Didcot, which has been transformed from a village into a town that will soon number sixty thousand people with a station used by three million commuters a year; and in the Earth Trust lands all around us that are part of the wider movement of nature reserves and national parks trying to preserve something of the peace and beauty of our countryside.

But the aspect of our view that most potently represents the last half-century in Britain's history is the view we have of the past, present and future of the energy supplies on which previous progress has been based and by which further progress is now threatened (Chapter *Power viewing*). Representing the past is the site of Didcot A, the coal-fired power station that burned millions of tons of pulverised coal every year for half a century. Representing the present, and our current dependence on natural gas, are the less prominent buildings of Didcot B. Cleaner than coal, maybe, but still a fossil fuel. To represent the future, we have a choice. Just visible to the naked eye, twenty miles to the west, stands the Westmill energy farm with its five slowly turning wind turbines and twenty thousand solar panels. But if a new and cleaner kind of mega power station is needed, then that, too, is represented in our view by the Culham Centre for Fusion Energy, two miles to the north. Here, teams of scientists and engineers are attempting to replicate on earth the process that powers the sun and the stars. If, in the years to come, they can solve the problems of scaling up the fusion process then cheap, clean, safe and almost limitless energy will be within reach.

We are now almost at the end of the history of England as seen from these modest hills rising from the Oxfordshire plain. But history, we hope, never ends. And from this remarkable viewpoint, it may also be possible to see something of our future.

Four miles to the south-west of the Clumps is something that looks like a film set for Star Wars – a giant silver doughnut set in the middle of the countryside. This is Britain's national synchrotron, also known as the Diamond Light Source, around which electrons can be accelerated to almost the speed of light, generating beams ten billion times brighter than the sun. At various points around the circuit, the beamlines are deflected into laboratories where scientists use them to study in unimaginable detail anything from fragments of ancient papyrus to the structure of a virus or a vaccine.

The Diamond Light Source is part of a Harwell Science and Innovation Campus that has long been home to the UK space industry but has also now become one of the greatest centres of scientific research and development anywhere in the world. Here, on seven hundred acres of land where Iron Age families once grew their crops, six thousand people from sixty countries are building on the achievements of the past to create or protect the future. In the more than two hundred commercial enterprises and government institutions on the Harwell campus, progress is being made in artificial intelligence and machine learning, in vaccine development and distribution, in overcoming antibiotic resistance, in reducing radiation dangers in space vehicles, in safely decommissioning nuclear power stations, in developing more precisely targeted anti-cancer drugs, in strengthening cybersecurity, in finding ways to bring digital technologies to the world's poorest communities, in handling data from the CERN Large Hadron Collider in Geneva, in making lighter and longer-lasting batteries, in designing all-terrain robots and cargo drones, in devising ways of sweeping space of the debris that litters the orbital highway, in analysing light spectra to learn about the exoplanets of other stars, and in researching satellite technologies for tracking ships, planes, weather patterns, crop yields and climate change here on earth. This extraordinary centre of science and innovation will soon be even more visible; over the next few years, it is scheduled to more than double in size.

With Harwell and its glimpse of the future, this walk through England's story as seen from the Wittenham Clumps comes to an end. There are of course many places in our country from which reminders of its history can be seen. But there can be few views in which so many different chapters of that history are represented. From the Iron Age fort under our feet to one of the world's leading centres for fusion research, from the Saxon Kings who first made England to the place where its Common Law was first codified, from the coming of the Age of Rail to the hope of fusion power, we may stand here and gaze on a landscape of time as well as place. It matters not what route you take around the clumps of beech trees atop Round and Fort Hills – on a clear day, you can see five thousand years.

NOTES

Part I

[1] Daniel Defoe, *A Tour thro' the Whole Island of Great Britain, 1724–27*.

[2] Faujas de Saint Fond, *Voyage en Angleterre*, 1797.

[3] A polecat was known to be living in Wittenham Wood in 1898.

[4] R. N. Morris and J. Mogey, *The Sociology of Housing, Studies at Berinsfield*, Routledge & Kegan Paul (1965).

[5] Francis Bernard's ownership of Mount Desert Island off the coast of Maine was legitimate in that it was given to him by the Massachusetts Assembly soon after he became Governor. Today, the hundred-square-mile island is the home of the Acadia National Park, whose fashionable summer resorts and scenic landscape attract more than two million tourists a year. Francis Bernard's son, John, was allowed to inherit half the island.

[6] James Otis, *c.* 12 Sept. 1768, quoted in *The Papers of Francis Bernard, Governor of Colonial Massachusetts, 1760-69*, ed. Colin Nicolson, 6 vols., (Boston, 2007–), vol. 4 (1768) (Boston, 2015), 299.

[7] *Revolutionary Characters*, the website from which this is quoted, is a program of Revolutionary Spaces, 310 Washington Street, Boston, MA 02109. www.revolutionarycharacters.org

[8] The village of Brightwell, which became Brightwell-cum-Sotwell in 1946, was in Berkshire at the time. It was transferred to Oxfordshire in 1974.

[9] Following a boundary change in 1974, the Wittenham Clumps are now in the county of Oxfordshire.

[10] The trees on Brightwell Barrow were planted by the landowner William Toovey in 1840, approximately a hundred years after the planting of the Wittenham Clumps. They were originally known as Toovey's Folly.

Part II

[11] Brightwell was re-named Brightwell-cum-Sotwell in 1946. It lies just to the south of the Wittenham Clumps and is today in the county of Oxfordshire.

[12] Hewitt, H. J. 1899. Notes and Queries. *The Berks, Bucks and Oxon Archaeological Journal, 4 (4): 124*

[13] There seems to be an interesting exception to this finding. Many people have experienced the state that the psychologist Mihaly Csikszenmnihaly called 'flow', in which, during a prolonged period of intense concentration – whether on a game of chess or writing a book – there comes a point when one is so absorbed that one is no longer conscious of the effort required, or of the temptation to desist, and so will power is no longer required. The same phenomenon seems to also apply to sportsmen and women putting themselves through demanding physical and mental effort. The term 'flow' applies to both, though in sport it is usually described as being 'in the zone'.

[14] The first foot ('Season') is a trochee, the most commonly used variant in pentameter verse.

[15] Reports of tame foxes, often from animal rescue centres, usually mean that the brain of the fox has been damaged by a parasite rendering the fox unafraid of humans.

Part III

[16] S. J. C Taylor, *Church And State In England In The Mid-Eighteenth Century: The Newcastle Years 1742-1762*, submitted for the degree of Doctor of Philosophy in the University of Cambridge, 1987. Available online in The University in Society, Volume 1: Oxford and Cambridge from the 14th to the Early 19th Century.

[17] The Rector of Aston Tirrold in the mid-eighteenth century was Sir John Hoskyns, whose restoration of the parish church destroyed the mediaeval wall paintings in the transept and also the ancient box pews which Sir John disliked because 'The want of reverence was grievous, and the encouragement of sleep very great.'

[18] Trollope apparently took the name of Quiverfull from Psalm 127:3-5, in which a man with many children is referred to as having a quiver full of arrows. In the twentieth century, the Quiverfull movement promoted the idea that many children were part of God's purpose and that contraception was consequently a sin.

[19] Tithes were often of two kinds: large and small. The large tithe was paid on the main bulk output from the land – principally grain, hay and wood. Everything else was the small tithe. Sometimes the lay owner of the living kept the large tithes and the parson, like Mr Elton in *Sense and Sensibility*, kept the small tithe. Others in Jane Austen's repertoire of clergymen were Rectors – like Mr Collins and Edward Ferrars – and so were entitled to all the tithes of the parish, great and small.

[20] *The Guardian*, Wed 29 Nov 2017

[21] When a motion to grant women full undergraduate status came before the University Senate, an editorial in the *Cambridge Review* argued: 'Not that we wish in any way to appear unchivalrous or to minimise the good work often done by women students; but 'so long as the sun and moon endureth' Cambridge should remain a society for men.' The motion to admit women was defeated.

[22] *The Intellectuals and the Masses* (1992) and *What Good are the Arts* (2006), both published by Faber & Faber.

[23] In some cases, the effect of this may even be measurable. One study, for example, used surveys to gauge the perceived physical attractiveness of female volunteers who were then asked to attend fake appointments. The researchers recorded how long the women waited when no one showed up: on average, the length of time that women were prepared to wait varied according to how attractive they were judged to be.

[24] The Ash and the Beech By Richard Mabey, published by Vintage in 2013. © The Ash and The Beech 2013. Reproduced by permission of Sheil Land Associates Ltd.

Part IV

[25] Ammianus Marcellinus, quoted in Peter Berresford Ellis *A Brief History of the Celts*, Hachette, 2013.

[26] St Birinus is said to have preached his first sermon on Churn Hill, also visible from the Clumps on the Berkshire Downs above Blewbury.

[27] The Conqueror crossed the Thames at Wallingford because the direct route to London was more heavily defended.

[28] Wigod's daughter, Aldgitha, was later married to one of the knights who sailed with William the Conqueror.

[29] In 2021, Wallingford Museum plans to unveil a scale model of Wallingford Castle as it might have looked in the mid-fourteenth century. Constructed by model maker Ben Taggart, and drawing on fifteen years of research by a multi-disciplinary team, the 1.5 x 1.6 metre model will show the walls, moats, drawbridges, and known buildings such as the great hall, kitchens and stables.

[30] The database of slave owners, compiled by University College London, lists thirty-two individuals in Oxfordshire (including five clergymen) and seventy-one in Berkshire who were compensated for the loss of their West Indian slaves following the Slavery Abolition Act of 1833.

[31] Blackstone also represents his times in less enlightened ways. For example, he accepted the traditional right of husbands to 'correct and chastise' their wives by corporal punishment. But recognising that this, like so much else in the common law, was too vague to be of use in legal judgements, he suggested that husbands could beat their wives with a stick providing the stick was 'no thicker than the husband's thumb'. Thankfully, the law has gone. Though we still have the rule of thumb.

[32] Named after a mythical 'Captain Swing' and thought to refer to the swinging stick with which crops had traditionally been hand threshed.